DISSOLVING DOLLARS

BY ALEX MARCHAND

WWW.DISSOLVINGDOLLARS.COM

D0912508

WRITING, ART, AND LETTERING
ALEX MARCHAND

ISBN-13: 978-144141-397-0
ISBN-10: 1-44141-397-9

451° Publishing

Fifth Print: June 2011
First Print: November 2008

EXPOSING THE DEBT-BASED INSANITY BEHIND MODERN MONEY

"I sincerely believe that banking establishments are more dangerous than standing armies, and that the principle of spending money to be paid by posterity, under the name of funding, is but swindling futurity on a large scale."

"I predict future happiness for Americans if they can prevent the government from wasting the labors of the people under the pretense of taking care of them."

THOMAS JEFFERSON

CONTENTS

PREFACE

There are a few books that deal with the same topics covered in this book. However, unlike those other books, this book is designed for people who would prefer something more direct, efficient, and simple than a standard, thick, text-filled book. Consequently, this book keeps things casual and to the point using an informal, non-threatening, visually intriguing comic-book-like format; it is like Cliffs Notes for understanding modern money.

This book's format mockingly subverts the tradition of hiding this kind of subject matter in an air of dry inaccessibility. So, in this book, you won't find things like seemingly impressive yet ultimately incestuous webs of footnotes and endnotes citing people like so-called economists. You'll just find the facts—all laid out in an easy to follow format. (Note: Most economists either work for Wall Street or the government and so their economics are skewed to favor their employers' objectives. That is how they get and keep their jobs.)

The modern monetary system is a very important subject that very few people understand (including people who are supposed to understand). If people understood the modern monetary system, reforming it would be the most pressing issue of the day. The biggest fallacy held by most people concerning money today is the belief that the government creates U.S. dollars. The government merely creates coins and debt. That is why the government is over 12 trillion dollars in debt and pays around a half a trillion dollars a year in interest on that debt. Private banks are who create U.S. dollars, and they create them out of debt (loans). Hence, money in the modern world is made out of debt. No debt essentially means no money.

Although this book is primarily designed as a gateway book to the truth about the monetary system, it also works as a good refresher book. This book is meant to be the kind of book a person can quickly and easily read over and over again and look back upon until everything sinks in. So, enjoy, study, and then share.

AS A COMPLIMENT TO THIS BOOK, VISIT
WWW.DISSOLVINGDOLLARS.COM

IT'S A PYRAMID SCHEME
WHERE INDEBTEDNESS FEEDS ON MORE INDEBTEDNESS.

MONEY IS CREATED AT THE TOP OF THE PYRAMID OUT OF THIN AIR AS DEBT BY THE BIG BANKS HEADED BY THE FEDERAL RESERVE.

THEN THE MONEY FLOWS DOWN THE PYRAMID TO SOAK INTEREST PAYMENTS BACK UP THE PYRAMID TO THOSE AT THE TOP.

MULTINATIONAL CORPORATIONS

STATES/GOVERNMENTS

SMALLER BANKS/BUSINESS

WAGE EARNERS/TAXPAYERS/THE INDEBTED

MORE + THE COST OF BORROWING MONEY – LESS

IT IS FACILITATED BY:
* FRACTIONAL RESERVE BANKING
* DEBT/INTEREST
* GOVERNMENT SUPPORT

WHEN THE PYRAMID BECOMES TOO TOP HEAVY, IT TOPPLES OVER.

0

CHAPTER ZERO

ITRODUCTION

IT IS WELL ENOUGH THAT PEOPLE OF THE NATION DO NOT UNDERSTAND OUR BANKING AND MONETARY SYSTEM, FOR IF THEY DID, I BELIEVE THERE WOULD BE A REVOLUTION BEFORE TOMORROW MORNING.

HENRY FORD
AUTOMOBILE INDUSTRIALIST
(1863 – 1947)

Most people are somehow led to believe that a subject like the nature of the monetary system is too boring, too complex, or just too inconsequential to bother understanding. But it isn't—especially if you are a person who doesn't like having your money stolen from you.

You see, the modern monetary system is basically a big scam, and to add insult to injury, it is cursed with a fatal flaw. Yet, the fatal flaw is rarely, if ever, addressed. People address the ever-growing symptoms of the fatal flaw, and they try to tame

1

those symptoms with things like bailouts, regulation, and interest rate adjustments. However, the fatal flaw itself is ignored. Thus, as time passes, the fatal flaw only becomes ever more magnified. The flaw is fixable. Yet, the flaw is facilitated by every person who uses the system while not understanding how it works.

% $1 %

The United States has been in various stages of credit default for many decades now. But it has been saved so far by the fact that the dollar still acts as the world's reserve currency. Decades ago, a paper dollar was redeemable for an ounce of silver (or a fraction of an ounce of gold). Today, a dollar is redeemable for a dollar of debt. Or, in other words, a dollar represents a dollar of debt. The bulk of the money supply is made by private banks through lending. Lending means debt, and with debt comes interest. To make the money to pay interest requires more dollars and more debt. This creates an explosive feedback loop of ever-growing debt requiring ever more dollars for interest. And therein rests the fatal flaw of the system: this ever-growing debt inevitably means ever more dollars, and ever more dollars only works if there is ever more growth to absorb those dollars.

2

Growth requires ample resources and energy. Otherwise, growth can't keep up. But that makes growth taxing on the environment (limited resources). If growth can't keep up with ever more dollars, that means a progressive dissolving of their value. Dissolving dollars make past debts worth less and act as a form of taxation. Consequently, indebted governments like dissolving dollars as an alternative to direct taxing. However, dissolving dollars are what is referred to as inflation—the symptom of which is rising prices (too much debt chasing too few goods and services). On the other hand, if the flow of ever more dollars were to stop or slow dramatically, the whole system would tumble into deep depression. A dissolving supply of dollars would kill growth, kill the economy, and mean a giant default on the entire debt system.

In that sense, the modern debt-based monetary system, in one way or another, amounts to a suicidal bender. And that bender is facilitated by the ignorance of the system's users to the perceived benefit of its operators (politicians and banking). Thus, change is dependent on knowledge.

The insane system can only operate under the shadow of ignorance. Therefore, the purpose of this book is to help illuminate that shadow.

THE MONEY SUPPLY IS MADE OF DEBT. WITH DEBT COMES INTEREST.

AS A RESULT, THE MONEY SUPPLY AND THE ECONOMY HAVE TO GROW FASTER THAN THE APPETITE OF EXPONENTIALLY GROWING DEBT AND INTEREST.

IF MONEY SUPPLY GROWTH AND ECONOMIC EXPANSION DON'T KEEP UP, THE ECONOMY IS DESTROYED BY THE DEBT TORNADO. AND THAT MEANS DEPRESSION.

In the following pages, through words and illustrations, you will learn the story of how the modern debt-based monetary system came about, how it works, and what can be done to change it—to avert both personal and collective disaster.

CHAPTER ONE
WHAT IS MONEY?

In order to understand the modern debt-based money system, we first need to understand what money is. Put simply, money is anything that is socially and or legally accepted as payment for goods, services, and the settlement of debt; it is a store of value.

THERE ARE FOUR MAIN TYPES OF MONEY:

* COMMODITY MONEY *

* REPRESENTATIVE MONEY *

* CREDIT MONEY *

* FIAT MONEY *

5

COMMODITY MONEY

Commodity money is money that can be used for trade, but has its own intrinsic value as a commodity. So, for instance, corn could be used as commodity money. But it wouldn't be very practical. You would need to push wheelbarrows full of corn around with you to buy most things. Plus, corn has a limited shelf life.

NOTE: THE WORD SALARY COMES FROM THE ROMANS. THEY USED SALT AS A FORM OF COMMODITY MONEY.

The most widely accepted form of money throughout recorded history has been the commodity money duo known as gold and silver. As early as 650 B.C., silver was used to make Greek coins. And around 560 B.C., gold coins were put to use in the Kingdom of Lydia, located in what is now western Turkey.

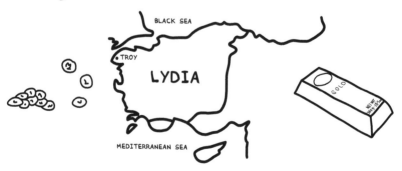

Since there is a relatively small and finite supply of gold and silver on the planet earth, and since extracting it takes some real labor, it is considered precious metal. A little bit of gold or silver holds quite a bit of value. Thus, that makes it a practical and portable commodity to use as a means of exchange in most situations.

FUN FACT:

It is estimated that all the gold ever mined in history, if it were consolidated into one big cube, would measure only about 66 feet per side.

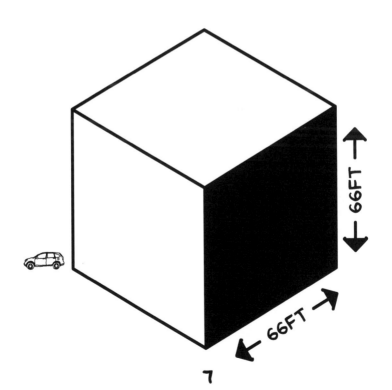

66FT

66FT

REPRESENTATIVE MONEY

Representative money is money that represents a fixed amount of a given commodity, like gold or oil. Carrying around and storing an actual physical commodity to use as money can be problematic. For instance, although gold is a more practical commodity to use for money than say corn, it is still easier to carry around something like a paper certificate redeemable for gold than actual gold.

REPRESENTATIVE MONEY AND FRACTIONAL RESERVE BANKING

In the old days, people deposited gold and silver coins with goldsmiths. The goldsmiths charged a fee to keep the gold and silver safely stored. In turn, goldsmiths gave people certificates redeemable for the deposited gold and silver. As these certificates became ever more acceptable as currency, there was ever less demand to withdraw gold and silver. People were happy to just use the certificates instead of the actual metal.

So, eventually, the goldsmiths got the bright idea that, instead of charging a storage fee for storing people's gold and silver, they could lend out, at interest, the unused gold and silver sitting in storage. People would never know or care, unless they all tried to withdraw their gold and silver at once (which is known as a bank run). So, the goldsmiths started just inventing money from thin air by issuing more certificates than the amount of gold and silver in reserve. Hence, the name fractional reserve banking (which is the cornerstone of modern banking). These extra certificates were loaned out to people at interest. In theory, once the loan was paid back, the goldsmiths would have the gold and silver represented by the certificates plus interest. But that is just theory because, as you'll eventually see in this book, in a system like fractional reserve banking, things get very complex and very abstract very quickly.

FRACTIONAL RESERVE BANKING AT A 1:2 RATIO

THE RATIO OF RESERVES TO CERTIFICATES CAN BE ANY NUMBER. HISTORICALLY, A 1:10 RATIO HAS PROVEN ADEQUATE UNDER NORMAL CIRCUMSTANCES.

LEGITIMATE BANKING
1:1 RATIO

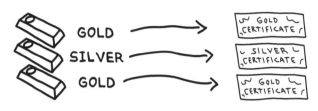

GOLD $\longrightarrow$ GOLD CERTIFICATE

SILVER $\longrightarrow$ SILVER CERTIFICATE

GOLD $\longrightarrow$ GOLD CERTIFICATE

RESERVES

CERTIFICATES

CREDIT MONEY

Credit money is basically an IOU (I owe you) or promissory note. Bonds are an example of credit money. Credit money is based on future payment. There is an element of risk to credit money; it might not be paid, and it might not be worth as much upon redemption as when issued. That risk is why credit money carries with it interest.

LEVERAGE: LEVERAGE IS THE PRACTICE OF USING A SMALL AMOUNT OF MONEY TO CONTROL A LARGER AMOUNT OF MONEY, OFTEN THROUGH DEBT (CREDIT MONEY). FOR EXAMPLE, IF A PERSON TOOK OUT A LOAN TO BUY A $100,000 HOUSE WITH A DOWN PAYMENT OF $10,000, THAT PERSON WOULD BE LEVERAGED 10 TO 1. IF THAT PERSON TURNED AROUND AND SOLD THE HOUSE FOR $110,000, THAT WOULD MEAN THE PERSON WOULD MAKE A 100% PROFIT ON THE $10,000 PUT DOWN TO BUY THE HOUSE. CONVERSELY, TURNING AROUND AND SELLING THE HOUSE FOR $90,000 WOULD MEAN A 100% LOSS. LEVERAGE MAGNIFIES BOTH GAINS AND LOSSES. (FRACTIONAL RESERVE BANKING IS A FORM OF LEVERAGE.)

FIAT MONEY

The final type of money is fiat money. The value of fiat money is determined by legal means (legal tender laws). In other words, fiat money is anything the government says is money. For instance, if the government says an IOU is money, then it is money. The major currencies of the contemporary world are fiat money.

↗ INFLATION AND DEFLATION ↘

Once you have an established form of money, the supply of that money dictates whether an economy experiences inflation or deflation. In general, the more money the less valuable it becomes. When the money supply expands excessively (faster than a proportionate increase in goods and services), that causes prices to rise and thus inflation. In deflation, the opposite occurs: the supply of money is decreased.

A SIMPLE INFLATION DEFLATION EXAMPLE

MONEY SUPPLY AND THE PRICE OF A CUP OF COFFEE

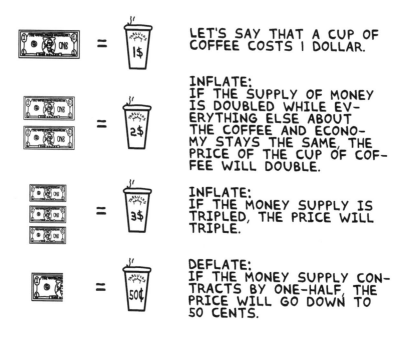

LET'S SAY THAT A CUP OF COFFEE COSTS 1 DOLLAR.

INFLATE:
IF THE SUPPLY OF MONEY IS DOUBLED WHILE EVERYTHING ELSE ABOUT THE COFFEE AND ECONOMY STAYS THE SAME, THE PRICE OF THE CUP OF COFFEE WILL DOUBLE.

INFLATE:
IF THE MONEY SUPPLY IS TRIPLED, THE PRICE WILL TRIPLE.

DEFLATE:
IF THE MONEY SUPPLY CONTRACTS BY ONE-HALF, THE PRICE WILL GO DOWN TO 50 CENTS.

This is a very simplified example; it doesn't factor in the complexities of debt money or the tendency of supply to increase with demand. However, in general, with deflation or inflation, dollars either dissolve in quantity or in value.

CHAPTER TWO

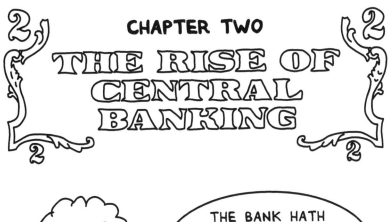

THE RISE OF CENTRAL BANKING

THE BANK HATH BENEFIT OF INTEREST ON ALL MONEYS WHICH IT CREATES OUT OF NOTHING.

SIR WILLIAM PATTERSON (1658-1719)
FOUNDER OF THE BANK OF ENGLAND

THE SPLIT TALLY STICK SYSTEM

The story of modern money starts in Europe. The British Empire was built using something called the Split Tally Stick System. The Split Tally Stick System was a monetary system first devised and implemented by King Henry upon assuming the throne of England in the year 1100. The Split Tally Stick System lasted nearly 800 years.

Polished sticks of wood with notches carved into them were split into two pieces. The one half was kept as a proof against counterfeiting and the other half was broken up and spent into the economy by the king. Since taxes could be paid using tally stick money, that made it demanded and acceptable.

THE SPLIT TALLY STICK SYSTEM

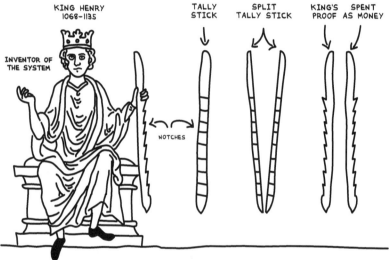

KING HENRY
1068-1135

TALLY STICK

SPLIT TALLY STICK

KING'S PROOF

SPENT AS MONEY

INVENTOR OF THE SYSTEM

NOTCHES

The tally stick system operated alongside gold and silver. But unlike gold and silver, the tally stick money was outside the control of private bankers (goldsmiths). However, usury laws, which limited interest charges, were relaxed by King Henry the 8th in the 1500s. And that suddenly allowed the bankers to accumulate a lot of wealth fast.

WHAT IS USURY? USURY IS PREDATORY LENDING, SUCH AS IN THE LENDING OF MONEY AT EXCESSIVE IN- TEREST RATES. IN ANTIQUITY, THE WHOLE CONCEPT OF MAKING MONEY OFF MONEY WAS CONSIDERED USURY AND WAS CONSIDERED UNACCEPTABLE.

INTEREST IS PROBLEMATIC; THERE IS NEVER ENOUGH MONEY IN A MONEY SYSTEM TO PAY INTEREST WITH- OUT INTRODUCING NEW MONEY (OR HAVING THE DEBTOR WORK DIRECTLY FOR THE CREDITOR). ALSO, INTEREST MAKES IT EASY FOR PEOPLE WHO ALREADY HAVE MONEY TO ACCUMULATE EVEN MORE MONEY SIMPLY DUE TO THE SAKE OF ALREADY HAVING IT.

This wealth helped back Oliver Cromwell in the English Revolution. After which, a long string of wars ensued. These wars were financed by the bankers, which made them even wealthier. However, while the bankers got rich, Britain found itself in financial ruin.

Britain's resulting indebtedness from all the war led to the formation of the Bank of England in 1694. The Bank of England was the result of a deal worked out between the desperate government and the eager private bankers. Since governments have the ability to tax and since governments can spend extremely large amounts of mon- ey, governments were recognized by bank- ers as the ideal entity upon which to loan money. With the formation of The Bank of England, the bankers got control over is- suing Britain's money, and the government got the ability to borrow all the money it wanted at interest from the bank.

It took a while, but The Bank of England finally did away with the old tally stick system completely by 1826. In 1834, a great fire occurred that destroyed most of the Palace of Westminster. The fire was the result of trying to incinerate a large stock of old tally sticks. This fire was immortalized in a series of paintings by J.M.W. Turner who witnessed the event.

THE BURNING OF THE HOUSES OF LORDS AND COMMONS, OCTOBER 16, 1834

J.M.W. TURNER
THE CLEVELAND MUSEUM OF ART

CENTRAL BANKING

The Bank of England was the first central bank, and as it turns out, it wasn't the last. The combination of public ignorance, private profiteering, and the appetite of governments to spend more money than they take in through taxes has in turn made central banking the cornerstone of modern money.

We will look at the contemporary, American version of this kind of system later on in the book. But first, we need to look at how central banking sculpted the history of The United States.

CHAPTER TWO

AMERICA'S MONEY

Upon the formation of the Bank of England, Britain's money supply increased substantially. And since that money was made from debt, Britain's debt grew substantially too. Britain's debt had grown from £1,250,000 in 1694 to £140,000,000 by the mid 1700s. With that huge and growing debt, Britain was in need of more revenue to service the interest on that debt.

Britain's new and prosperous America colonies were to be the source of the needed revenue. That meant taxation.

At the time, the America colonies were using a form of paper money called Colonial Scrip. Colonial Scrip was similar to the old, British tally stick money in that it was debt-free and issued directly by the government. The Pennsylvania version of Colonial Scrip proved to be a notably stable currency. Pennsylvania had its own public bank. Thus, Pennsylvania issued its currency by making loans secured by collateral like land. The interest on the loans (5%) was used as tax revenue, eliminating the need for taxes. The Pennsylvania system ended up keeping inflation controlled. The same cannot be said for other colonies at all times though. Nonetheless, scrip worked very well for the new colonies.

Ultimately, Ben Franklin attributed the prosperity of the new colonies to Colonial Scrip. Ben Franklin, who was a printer by trade, was a major advocate of paper money. However, Franklin's enthusiasm for scrip led to its downfall. Franklin took a trip to London in 1764. While in London, Franklin let a bit too much become known about Colonial Scrip. Colonial Scrip was a threat against the British bankers' monopoly on money.

Under pressure from the Bank of England, British parliament passed the Currency Act of 1764. The Currency Act made Colonial Scrip illegal and forced the colonies to make all tax payments to Britain in gold and silver.

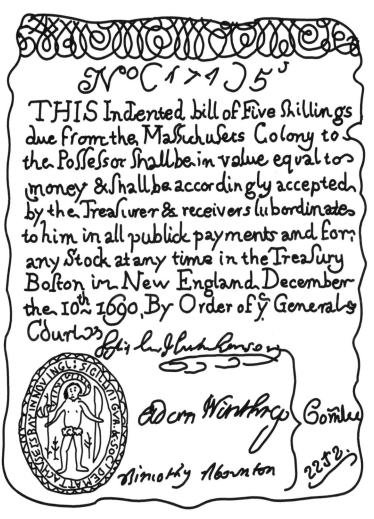

AN EXAMPLE OF COLONIAL SCRIP FROM MASSACHUSETTS 1690

Very quickly, prosperity turned to poverty in the America colonies. British taxation drained America of its gold and silver and increased debt. With this reversal of fortune, the waters of revolution were stirred.

IN ONE YEAR, THE CONDITIONS WERE SO REVERSED THAT THE ERA OF PROSPERITY ENDED, AND A DEPRESSION SET IN TO SUCH AN EXTENT THAT THE STREETS OF THE COLONIES WERE FILLED WITH UNEMPLOYED.

BENJAMIN FRANKLIN

The American Revolutionary War started in 1775, and it was funded by a new form of money called Continental Currency—issued by the Continental Congress. Since the colonies were now economically depressed and robbed of much of their gold and silver, there wasn't much faith behind Continental Currency. After malicious counterfeiting and thus runaway inflation, the currency ended up a failure, giving rise to the phrase, "not worth a continental."

One Third of a DOLLAR.

GEORGIA. N.HAMPS. MASSACHS. CONNICT. R.ISLAND. N.YORK. N.JERSEY. PENNSYLV. DELAWARE. MARYLAND. VIRGINIA. N.CAROL↑. S.CAROL↑.

AMERICAN CONGRESS.

WE ARE ONE

Printed by Hall & Sellers, in Philadelphia. 1776.

CONTINENTAL CURRENCY

Ultimately, Britain lost the war and America. But just because Britain lost America didn't mean banking interests lost America. The lure of private profits and the desire of politicians to spend other people's money meant it was just a matter of time until Central Banking came to America.

21

THE BANK OF NORTH AMERICA

In 1781, with the Continental Congress desperate for money, Financial Superintendent Robert Morris was allowed to form the first central bank of the new United States. Modeled after The Bank of England, this bank was called The Bank of North America. The government put up most of the money for the bank and then private interests proceeded to profit from the bank through fractional reserve money creation. After four years of currency depreciation, the bank's charter was not renewed. It was evident that this first attempt at central banking was not helping America.

THE CONSTITUTION

At the Constitutional Convention in 1787, a consistent agreement concerning how to handle the new nation's money was not so easy to come by. The failure of the Continental Currency made people paranoid about paper money. However, the Continental's failure was mostly a product of malicious counterfeiting by the British. After all, Colonial Scrip had worked well until the British made it illegal. Nonetheless, due to paper money paranoia, the United States

Constitution ended up a bit less than detailed on the subject of money.

Article 1, Section 8 of the Constitution enumerates the powers of the government. In regards to money, it reads the following:

The Congress shall have Power . . .

*To borrow money on the credit of the United States;

*To coin money, regulate the value thereof, and of foreign coin, and fix the Standard of Weights and Measures;

*To provide for the punishment of counterfeiting the securities and current coin of the United States;

Furthermore, Article I Section 10 of the Constitution reads that no state shall "emit bills of credit [or] make anything but gold and silver coin a tender in payment of debts."

WHAT IS LEGAL TENDER? IT IS SOMETHING THAT, BY LAW, CANNOT BE REFUSED IN THE SETTLEMENT OF A DEBT. SOMETHING LIKE A PIECE OF PAPER WITH A PICTURE OF A DEAD PRESIDENT ON IT IS ONLY CONSIDERED MONEY BECAUSE IT IS MADE SO BY GOVERNMENT LAW OR FIAT (DECREE).

So, the Constitution simply says that congress has the power to "coin" money and borrow money. And while it says that states can't make anything but gold and silver legal money, it doesn't explicitly say that the federal government can't (or that it can). The Constitution doesn't even define what a dollar is. To get an idea of the definition of a dollar, you need to look at the Coinage Act of 1792. In the Coinage Act, a dollar is linked to a certain weight and grade of silver based on a Spanish dollar. So, overall, without paying homage to context, the Constitution leaves a bit more wiggle room for biased interpretation about money than it probably should.

SKELETON KEY TO THE U.S. CONSTITUTION

You sort of kind of can do this or that; all you have to do is say, the Constitution implies it.

THE FIRST BANK OF
THE UNITED STATES

The Constitution's wiggle room concerning money soon opened the door to the formation of a new central bank in 1791. The new bank was pushed through congress by Treasury Secretary Alexander Hamilton. Although it took a year of debate, congress finally gave a 20-year charter to the new bank. The bank was named the First Bank of the United States. The bank printed bank notes in exchange for government debt (bonds). The bank facilitated the false impression that the notes the bank printed up were backed by gold. However, the bank was really just an elaborate form of making paper money; it was a compromise between government and private players invested in the bank to make a paper currency out of bank notes.

Although the central bank helped control the money system, it nonetheless was problematic. The bank loaned the government money, which made interest-bearing debt. And, using fractional reserve lending, the bank ran up the supply of money. In the bank's first five years of existence, inflation was 42%. The government could have just printed its own money debt free. But with the bank, private players got to profit off debt interest.

I WISH IT WERE POSSIBLE TO OBTAIN A SINGLE AMENDMENT TO OUR CONSTITUTION-- TAKING FROM THE FEDERAL GOVERNMENT THEIR POWER OF BORROWING.

PRESIDENT
THOMAS
JEFFERSON

IF THE AMERICAN PEOPLE EVER ALLOW PRIVATE BANKS TO CONTROL THE ISSUE OF THEIR CURRENCY, FIRST BY INFLATION, THEN BY DEFLATION, THE BANKS AND THE CORPORATIONS WHICH GROW UP AROUND THEM WILL DEPRIVE THE PEOPLE OF ALL PROPERTY UNTIL THEIR CHILDREN WAKE UP HOMELESS ON THE CONTINENT THEIR FATHERS CONQUERED.

After 20 years, in 1811, the charter on the First Bank of the United States was not renewed. Soon after that, The War of 1812 was instigated. To fund the war, the government encouraged reckless banking practices with banks buying war bonds and turning them into bank notes. By 1814, the war ended in a draw.

THE SECOND BANK OF
THE UNITED STATES

Although the First Bank of the United States was gone, the private interests bent on capitalizing off control of U.S. money were persistent. Thus, with the banking system in disorder, due to financing The War of 1812, that gave an excuse to push for a new central bank. In 1816, the Second Bank of the United States was formed and given a 20-year charter. Once again, it was the same old bank with just a different name.

JACKSON
AND THE BANK

Andrew Jackson was a staunch opponent of central banking. In 1828, he became president. But unfortunately, the charter on the Second Bank of the United States wasn't scheduled to run out until 1836.

Before Jackson's re-election in 1832, the bank actually tried to renew its charter four years early. The charter made it to Jackson's desk, at which point he vehemently vetoed it. Unable to get the votes in congress to override the veto, it held. Thus, the bank remained vulnerable to Jackson.

JACKSON & NO BANK 32

Jackson won re-election against Henry Clay by a landslide in 1832. And upon his re-election, he ordered the start of systematic withdraw of government funds from the bank. However, he had to go through a string of treasury secretaries before he found one with the fortitude to follow his orders.

The head of the bank, Nicholas Biddle, was not at all pleased with Jackson's actions. Biddle actually threatened to reduce the money supply and cause a depression if congress didn't cater to the bank. Sure enough, soon a depression was brought upon the country by the bank calling in loans and refusing to issue new loans. Biddle blamed Jackson on the depression, saying it was caused by Jackson pulling out money from the bank. Nonetheless, by 1834, the Second Bank of the United States was dying. With the bank dying, in 1835, Jackson was able to pay off the national debt. He was the only president to ever do that. In 1836, the bank's charter was not renewed.

The bank completely ceased operations in 1841.

PRESIDENT
ANDREW JACKSON

THE BOLD EFFORT(S) THE PRESENT BANK HAD MADE TO CONTROL THE GOVERNMENT...ARE BUT PREMONITIONS OF THE FATE THAT AWAITS THE AMERICAN PEOPLE SHOULD THEY BE DELUDED INTO A PERPETUATION OF THIS INSTITUTION OR THE ESTABLISHMENT OF ANOTHER LIKE IT.

Although Jackson killed the central bank, state chartered, private banks were still using fractional reserve banking to issue bank notes. However, now, without centralization, there wasn't a means of centrally manipulating the economy. What Alexander Hamilton attempted to do with central banking had merits. Unfortunately, private interests (including foreign, private interests) let in too much room for manipulation of both the economy and the government.

LINCOLN'S GREENBACKS

When the Civil War broke out in 1861, over economic inequality between the north and south, President Lincoln was in need of money to fund the war efforts. The bankers love war, because war means debt. Thus, the bankers were eager to loan Lincoln money. But the interest rates they proposed were exorbitant, 24% to 36%. Consequently, Lincoln looked for other means to fund the war. The solution eventually brought to him was to print full legal tender debt-free treasury notes. These notes were later called greenbacks, due to the green ink used on the back to distinguish them from other notes. Since the money was required by government fiat to be acceptable currency, people had no choice but to use the money. But the bankers didn't like the idea one bit. So, they had some limitations put on the notes: the notes couldn't be used to pay import duties or interest on the national debt.

Between 1862 and 1865, greenbacks totaling $450,000,000 were printed. But in 1863, in need of congressional approval to print more greenbacks, Lincoln was forced to compromise with the bankers. This led to the National Banking Act of 1863, which was modified in 1864. The act made National Banks, National Bank Notes, and helped sell bonds to fund the war.

A GREENBACK FROM 1862

THIS IS WHAT A PROPAGANDA PIECE IN THE TIMES OF LONDON HAD TO SAY ABOUT LINCOLN'S GREENBACKS.

THE TIMES
London

If that mischievous financial policy, which had its origin in the North American Republic, should become indurated down to a fixture, then that government will furnish its own money without cost. It will pay off debts and be without a debt. It will have all the money necessary to carry on its commerce. It will become prosperous beyond precedent in the history of civilized governments of the world. The brains and the wealth of all countries will go to North America. That government must be destroyed or it will destroy every monarchy on the globe.

THE NATIONAL BANKING ACT

The National Banking Act, which emerged out of trying to fund the Civil War, was the first step in instituting what would eventually become the Federal Reserve System in 1913. With the new National Banks came a practice of explicitly basing money on government debt as reserves instead of reserves of gold and silver. In other words, money could be based on government bonds (treasuries). On notes of this nature it read, "Secured by United States Bonds." National banks were allowed to print bank notes equal to 90% of the value of the bonds that backed the notes. The notes were widely circulated and were accepted for the payment of taxes and duties.

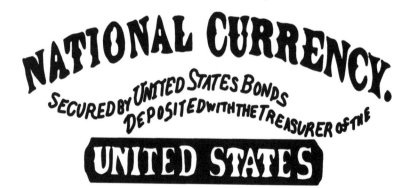

Since money could now be based on federal government bonds, the government had no choice but to carry a debt. To pay off the debt would mean a contraction of the money supply.

In 1865, an act was passed that imposed a 10% tax on state bank notes. That forced state bank notes out of circulation and increased the number of National Banks (1,644 by 1866).

THE GOVERNMENT SHOULD CREATE, ISSUE, AND CIRCULATE ALL THE CURRENCY AND CREDIT NEEDED TO SATISFY THE SPENDING POWER OF THE GOVERNMENT AND THE BUYING POWER OF CONSUMERS. THE PRIVILEGE OF CREATING AND ISSUING MONEY IS NOT ONLY THE SUPREME PREROGATIVE OF GOVERNMENT, BUT IT IS THE GOVERNMENT'S GREATEST CREATIVE OPPORTUNITY. THE FINANCING OF ALL PUBLIC ENTERPRISE, AND THE CONDUCT OF THE TREASURY WILL BECOME MATTERS OF PRACTICAL ADMINISTRATION. MONEY WILL CEASE TO BE MASTER AND WILL THEN BECOME SERVANT OF HUMANITY.

PRESIDENT
ABRAHAM LINCOLN

Since it was outside their control, the bankers were committed to getting rid of the greenback. So, in 1866, the Contraction Act was passed. This reduced the number of greenbacks in circulation; in turn, it steadily reduced the amount of money in circulation in America. Getting rid of the greenback was the first step in the efforts of private bankers to take back control of America's money. Since gold exists in a limited supply, it is fairly easy to control. And since the bankers wanted control of America's money, instituting a gold standard was seen as an obtainable objective. The only kind of paper money the bankers were interested in was interest-bearing IOUs that they could control. Interest-free, debt-free greenbacks were the bankers' nightmare.

CONSPIRACY CORNER:
LINCOLN WAS ASSASSINATED IN 1865. SOME SPECULATE THAT LINCOLN'S GREENBACK POLICY PLAYED A KEY PART IN HIS ASSASSINATION.

THE SILVER PROBLEM

After bringing the greenback under control, the next obstacle was silver. The discovery of abundant silver in the American west made silver almost as threatening to the bankers' monopoly on money as the greenback. Under the current law, anyone could bring silver to the mint and have it coined. Consequently, the Coinage Act of 1873 was pushed through congress (known as "The Crime of 73"); it stopped the coinage of silver dollars. At the same time, in part to tame the influence of America's wealth of silver outside the United States, silver was demonetized in many other countries, such as Germany, France, Switzerland, Italy, Belgium, Norway, Denmark, Sweden, and the Netherlands. In the end, just about every major country had a gold standard imposed upon it by the bankers, except China.

After the banking interests brought both the greenback and silver under control, money supply in the United States dropped steadily and dramatically. Inflation was a big problem during the Civil War—due to the large influx of paper money to fund the war. But now, the problem was deflation. The new gold standard, combined with an increasing population (population doubled from 1860 to 1890), made the money supply shrink from $50 per person in 1866, to less than $15 per person in 1876. And it didn't stop there. Money supply shrunk to less than $7 per person by the 1880s.

This contraction in the money supply certainly didn't go unnoticed. In turn, a large movement to return to silver money arose. Consequently, in 1876, Congress put forth the United States Silver Commission. The report found that the demonetization of silver was beneficial to no one but the bankers.

THE UNITED STATES SILVER COMMISSION
1876

At the Christian era, the metallic money of the Roman Empire amounted to $1,800,000,000. By the end of the fifteenth century, it had shrunk to less than $200,000,000. During this period a most extraordinary and baleful change took place in the condition of the world. Population dwindled and commerce, arts, wealth, and freedom all disappeared. The people were reduced by poverty and misery to the most degraded conditions of serfdom and slavery. The disintegration of society was almost complete. The conditions of life were so hard, that individual selfishness was the only thing consistent with the instinct of self-preservation. All public spirit, all generous emotions, all the noble aspirations of man shriveled and disappeared as the volume of money shrunk and as prices fell...History records no such disastrous transition as that from the Roman Empire to the Dark Ages. Various explanations have been given of this entire breaking down of the framework of society, but it was certainly coincident with a shrinkage in the volume of money, which was also without historical parallel.

In 1878, under mounting public pressure, the Bland-Allison Act was passed by Congress. This allowed the minting of some silver coins again. But unlike before, people couldn't bring their own silver to the mint to be struck into coins. Thus, the silver supply was still controlled.

THE WONDERFUL WIZARD OF OUNCES

With gold dominant, monetary reform was a hot issue as the 19th century closed. In 1894, a Massillon, Ohio man named Jacob Coxey led a march of unemployed workers (known as Coxey's Army) on Washington D.C. demanding that the government print debt-free treasury notes (greenbacks) to fund infrastructure construction. Coxey's march is credited as being the inspiration for "The Wonderful Wizard of Oz" by L. Frank Baum, which can be read as an allegory on monetary reform efforts of the late 1800s.

Yellow Brick Road = Gold

Silver Slippers = Silver
(Changed to Ruby in the Film)

Wicked Witches = Banking Interests

Wicked Witch of the West =
McKinley, Rockefeller

Wicked Witch of the East =
J.P. Morgan, Wall Street,
Grover Cleveland

Scarecrow = Farmers

Tin Woodsman = Industrial Workers

Cowardly Lion = William Jennings Bryan. Bryan ran for president against William McKinley in 1896 and 1900. McKinley supported the gold monopoly and Bryan supported free silver. Bryan lost both elections.

Wizard of Oz = The President

Emerald City = Green (Paper) Money

↗ BOOMS AND BUSTS ↘

Having control of the money supply means having the ability to control deflation and inflation, and thus the ability to control the boom bust cycle. In the boom bust cycle, wealth is transferred. The people privy to the cycle are the ones to whom the wealth is transferred. In theory, the advantage of a central bank is that it should be able to avoid the boom bust cycle. But instead, since it synchronizes the economy, it exacerbates the boom bust cycle. Centralized control causes everything to happen at once, which both over-extends and over-retracts the system. The entire economy is simultaneously stimulated by making borrowing money easy and cheap; then it is reversed by making borrowing difficult and expensive. When this happens, a certain percentage of businesses, banks, and people fail. The strong players, who are most privy to the cycle, then come in and seize assets.

> WHOEVER CONTROLS THE VOLUME OF MONEY IN ANY COUNTRY IS ABSOLUTE MASTER OF ALL INDUSTRY AND COMMERCE... AND WHEN YOU REALIZE THAT THE ENTIRE SYSTEM IS VERY EASILY CONTROLLED, ONE WAY OR ANOTHER, BY A FEW POWERFUL MEN AT THE TOP, YOU WILL NOT HAVE TO BE TOLD HOW PERIODS OF INFLATION AND DEPRESSION ORIGINATE.

ASSASSINATED PRESIDENT
JAMES GARFIELD

DOLLAR TIMELINE 1792 TO 1900

1792 TO 1834: THE COINAGE ACT OF 1792 MADE THE DOLLAR BACKED BY A BI-METAL SYSTEM OF BOTH GOLD AND SILVER AT A RATIO OF 15:1.

1834 TO 1873: THE 15:1 RATIO WAS CHANGED TO A 16:1 RATIO AND THE WEIGHT OF THE NATION'S GOLD COINAGE WAS REDUCED.

1873 TO 1900: A SERIES OF ADJUSTMENTS WERE MADE DUE TO THE LARGE INFLUX OF SILVER ON THE MARKET COMING FROM LARGE SILVER DIS-COVERIES IN THE AMERICAN WEST.

* 1861: THE FEDERAL GOVERNMENT GOT DIRECTLY INVOLVED WITH LEGAL TENDER, PAPER MONEY STARTING WITH LINCOLN'S GREENBACKS. THIS LED TO NUMEROUS KINDS OF PAPER MONEY: TREASURY NOTES, NATIONAL BANK NOTES (BACKED BY GOVERNMENT BONDS), UNITED STATES NOTES, GOLD CERTIFICATES, SILVER CER-TIFICATES, AND ULTIMATELY FEDERAL RESERVE NOTES. SOME REISSUED GREEN-BACKS STAYED IN CIRCULATION INTO THE 1990S.

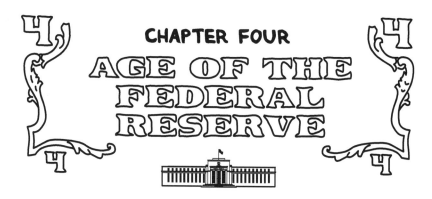

CHAPTER FOUR
AGE OF THE FEDERAL RESERVE

THE BIRTH

America's economy was roaring as the twentieth century began. In fact, it was doing so well that businesses were starting to use their big profits to expand without borrowing money from the banks. On top of that, the number of banks in the United States continued to expand. That was a problem because less than one third of those banks were National Banks. That meant that a large portion of money was outside the control of the main bankers who wanted no less than total control of the nation's money.

In 1907, there was a rash of bank failures known as the Panic of 1907. This panic, and its aftermath, was used as an excuse to form something called the National Monetary Commission. The chairman of this commission was a Senator from Rhode Island named Nelson Aldrich. As part of the commission, Aldrich went to Europe for two years to consult with the central banks of England, Germany, and France.

In 1910, after Aldrich completed his tour of Europe, he and seven of the richest men in America took a secretive trip to Jekyll Island, Georgia. The purpose of this trip was to sit down and figure out how to bring central banking back to the United States.

GEORGIA

JEKYLL ISLAND

The result of the trip was a bill called the Aldrich Bill. However, once proposed to congress, the bill was quickly recognized as a bill in the interest of the big bank-ers. Consequently, the bill was repackaged under the name, the Glass-Owen bill.

The New York Times

December 14, 1913

SENATOR ROOT SEES PERIL IN MONEY BILL

Measure Has Basic Defects of Bryan Doctrines, He Tells the Senate.

PICTURES VAST INFLATION

Says Prices Will Rise, Gold Vanish, Stocks Fall, Those Held Abroad Forced Home.

PAWNING NATION'S CREDIT

Vote on Bill Fixed for Next Thursday.

On December 23, 1913, with some Representatives and Senators already gone for Christmas holiday, the Glass-Owen bill was slipped through congress, and the Federal Reserve Act of 1913 was signed into law by President Wilson the next day. With the passage of this bill, a new central bank came into existence called the Federal Reserve. At that point, the bill wasn't everything the bankers wanted, but they figured that getting it signed into law was the most important thing. After that, they could steadily tweak the details to their exact preferences through amendments. And that is what they did.

PRESIDENT'S SIGNATURE - ENACTS CURRENCY LAW

Wilson Declares It the First of Series of Constructive Acts to Aid Business.

INCOME TAX: ON OCTOBER 3, 1913, THE FEDERAL INCOME TAX TARIFF ACT WAS SIGNED INTO LAW. UPON THE PRESUMED RATIFICATION OF THE SIXTEENTH AMENDMENT, FEDERAL INCOME TAX WAS IMPOSED UPON THE AMERICAN PEOPLE. THE INCOME TAX WAS SOLD TO THE PUBLIC AS A MEANS TO STICK IT TO THE RICH. BUT ITS TRUE SIGNIFICANCE RESTED IN THE ROLE IT WOULD PLAY IN KEEPING INTEREST ON GOVERNMENT DEBT PAID.

THE GREAT DEPRESSION

The 1920s were called the "Roaring Twenties" due to the large influx of money into the economy facilitated by rampant lending. At the same time, government debt was actually shrinking. The Federal Reserve was making loans to banks to expand the money supply. But eventually, the system became over extended enough that it was

43

time to start calling in all the debt. This started the Great Depression.

The Great Depression began with the Wall Street crash of October 1929. With the economic control of centralized banking in place, there came insider information. Thus, a lot of the big guys made big money by selling high and then buying back low.

The Great Depression ended up so great mostly due to the government and its growth of size and intervention. The government attempted to fix prices (wages) and keep them at their inflated 1920s levels—instead of letting the system cleanse itself of its excesses. Economic pain is politically unpopular. However, politicians and central banks are not smarter than the economy. The economy knows how to fix itself if left to operate without manipulations made possible by government conspiring with and against private enterprise.

THE DEPRESSION OF 1920: THERE WAS A DEPRESSION IN 1920 THAT IS RARELY EVER MENTIONED DUE TO THE FACT THAT THE GOVERNMENT DID NOTHING TO CONTROL IT. CONSEQUENTLY, WHILE IT WAS BRIEFLY DEVASTATING, IT WAS OVER ALMOST AS SOON AS IT STARTED.

Although the Great Depression didn't really end until after World War II, President Roosevelt's New Deal of infrastructure spending is often inaccurately credited as being what pulled the U.S. out of the Great Depression. The idea of the New Deal dated back to the 1890s and Jacob Coxey's march on Washington D.C. of unemployed workers demanding that the government print debt-free notes (greenbacks) to fund infrastructure construction. While Roosevelt's New Deal did include creating jobs through infrastructure construction, Roosevelt left out the most important part of Coxey's proposal. Roosevelt funded the New Deal (Raw Deal) by borrowing the money instead of having the government just issue its own debt-free notes.

ECONOMIST
MILTON FRIEDMAN

"THE FEDERAL RESERVE DEFINITELY CAUSED THE GREAT DEPRESSION BY CONTRACTING THE AMOUNT OF CURRENCY IN CIRCULATION BY ONE-THIRD FROM 1929 TO 1933."

* NATIONAL PUBLIC RADIO INTERVIEW (JAN 1996)

NOTE: THERE WAS A SEEMING CONTRACTION IN THE MONEY SUPPLY DURING THE DEPRESSION. BUT THAT WAS, FOR THE MOST PART, DUE TO A LACK OF FAITH IN THE BANKING SYSTEM CAUSING PEOPLE TO HOARD CASH. THE CONSEQUENT FEAR OF BANK RUNS, DUE TO LACK OF AMPLE DEPOSITS, MADE BANKS LEND MUCH MORE CAUTIOUSLY.

THE GOLD CONFISCATION OF 1933

Executive Order 6102 was signed on April 5, 1933 by U.S. President Franklin D. Roosevelt "Forbidding the Hoarding of Gold Coin, Gold Bullion, and Gold Certificates." It required all citizens to deliver on or before May 1, 1933, all gold coins, gold bullion, and gold certificates to the Federal Reserve. Since the Federal Reserve was under the fractional reserve gold standard at the time, the extra gold was proposed as a means to increase the money supply. A price of $20.67 was paid per ounce.

Then, in 1934, the fixed price for an ounce of gold was lifted to $35 per ounce. However, due to the limitations imposed on U.S. citizens owning gold (which lasted until 1974), only foreigners could sell gold to the Federal Reserve at this new price. By lifting the price of gold, the money supply was increased (but at the sacrifice of a 41% loss in the value of the dollar). From this came a kind of split gold standard in the sense that the U.S. dollar was only backed by gold on an international level and not a domestic level.

In 1936, the U.S. Bullion Depository at Fort Knox, Kentucky, was constructed to house the new abundance of gold. At its peak on

December 31, 1941, the depository held 649.6 million ounces of gold, which amounted to the majority of the world's gold reserves. Today, according to the U.S. mint, it only holds 147 million ounces.

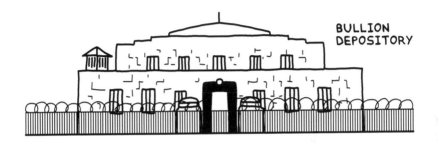

BULLION DEPOSITORY

THE BRETTON WOODS SYSTEM

In 1944, at the end of World War II, delegates from 44 Allied Nations met in Bretton Woods, New Hampshire to rebuild the international economic system. The stated objectives of the meeting were to assist international trade and stabilize currency exchange rates. Several things came out of the meeting, such as the World Bank, the International Monetary Fund, and a new international gold standard. In the Bretton woods agreement, the U.S. dollar was pegged to gold at $35 an ounce; in turn, the dollar eventually became the backing of much of the world's currencies, requiring countries to hold reserves of dollars.

THE END OF GOLD

U.S. gold reserves were shrinking fast by the 1970s. In a desire to compete with devalued foreign currencies without explicitly devaluing the dollar, in 1971, the United States suspended convertibility of gold for dollars. This ended the Bretton Woods System, and thus it ended any resemblance of a gold standard in the United States. Once the fixed gold price of $35 per ounce was removed, and restrictions on money supply growth were thus removed, the price of gold marched rapidly higher—until it peaked at $850 in 1980. (The $850 mark was well surpassed in 2008.)

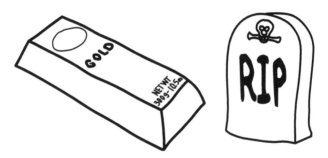

IMF DIGITAL GOLD: BY TAKING THE DOLLAR OFF THE GOLD STANDARD, THE INTERNATIONAL MONETARY FUND, WHICH WAS FORMED DURING THE BRETTON WOODS CONFERENCE, HAD MORE FREEDOM IN MAKING ITS BRAND OF INTERNATIONAL CURRENCY CALLED A SPECIAL DRAWING RIGHT (SDR). SDRS ARE MADE OF A BASKET OF MAJOR CURRENCIES USED IN INTERNATIONAL TRADE AND FINANCE. SDRS ACT AS A KIND OF DIGITAL GOLD STANDARD.

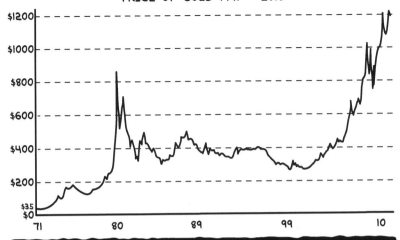

PRICE OF GOLD 1971 - 2010

DOLLAR TIMELINE
1900 TO PRESENT

1900 TO 1933: GOLD BECAME THE SOLE BACK-
ING OF THE DOLLAR, FIXED AT $20.67 PER
OUNCE.

1933 TO 1944: DURING THE GREAT DEPRES-
SION, GOLD WAS CONFISCATED FOR $20.67
PER OUNCE AND QUIETLY REPLACED BY A
SILVER STANDARD. DOLLARS BECAME CON-
VERTIBLE TO GOLD ONLY AT AN INTERNA-
TIONAL LEVEL, FIXED AT $35 PER OUNCE.

1944 TO 1963: THE BRETTON WOODS AGREE-
MENT MADE THE DOLLAR THE INTERNATIONAL
GOLD STANDARD.

1963 TO 1971: "WILL PAY TO THE BEARER ON
DEMAND" WAS REMOVED FROM ALL NEWLY
ISSUED FEDERAL RESERVE NOTES. CONVERT-
IBILITY OF DOLLARS TO SILVER CEASED, AND
COINS STOPPED CONTAINING SILVER.

1971 TO PRESENT: DOLLARS BECAME PURELY
FIAT CURRENCY (BACKED ONLY BY DEBT).

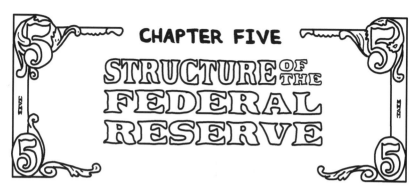

CHAPTER FIVE

STRUCTURE OF THE FEDERAL RESERVE

Now that we have a basic history of where the current monetary system came from, it is time to look at how it all works today.

The dollar is not on a gold or silver standard anymore, nor is it simply made by the government, like Lincoln's greenbacks. Instead, the modern dollar is best described as being on a debt standard. The value of a dollar is extracted from the commitment of the American people to pay off the debt that a dollar represents trough labor and productivity.

 ## THE FEDERAL RESERVE: PUBLIC OR PRIVATE?

The Federal Reserve (The Fed) isn't exactly public or private. Instead, it is best described as a cartel of private banks in partnership with the government. So, it is basically a government-supported, private banking cartel, which means it is validated by coercion. The cartel maximizes profits by reducing competition. And it ultimately distributes the risk inherent in the system to U.S. taxpayers, through things like bailouts, whenever the system starts to break down.

THE FED'S MAIN FUNCTIONS

THE MAIN FUNCTIONS OF THE MODERN FED DEVIATE NOTABLY FROM THOSE MANDATED IN THE ORIGINAL FEDERAL RESERVE ACT.

SERVES AS A CENTRAL BANK: It is the bank of banks and the government's bank. The U.S. Treasury has a checking account at the Fed. The U.S. Treasury, through its Bureau of Printing and Engraving, prints the nation's cash money supply at a fee to banks, and the Fed then distributes it to financial institutions.

CONTROLS THE MONEY SUPPLY: It does this by buying and selling treasury securities, adjusting reserve requirements (10%, 5%, 12% etc.), and by adjusting key interest rates—like the Federal Funds Rate, which is the rate banks charge each other for overnight loans of the reserves held by banks at the Fed.

ACTS AS LENDER OF LAST RESORT: It extends credit to troubled institutions —especially those whose failure could adversely impact the larger economy. Sometimes that means bailing out institutions at the ultimate expense of taxpayers. Direct Fed lending to banks is a monetary policy instrument called the Discount Window.

THE CARTEL STRUCTURE

The system is set up so that almost all power comes from the top to assure centralized control.

ONE - THE FED HEAD

The most public figure of the Federal Reserve is the Chairman of the Board of Governors.

RECENT FED HEADS

PAUL VOLCKER
(AUGUST 6, 1979 –
AUGUST 11, 1987)

ALAN GREENSPAN
(AUGUST 11, 1987 –
JANUARY 31, 2006)

BEN BERNANKE
(FEBRUARY 1, 2006 –)

TWO - BOARD OF GOVERNORS

The board of governors consists of seven members, including the chairman, that serve staggered 14-year terms (the chairman serves 4-year terms). They are appointed by the President (chosen from a list provided by the Fed) and are confirmed by the Senate. The board oversees the operations of the system, makes regulatory decisions, and sets reserve requirements.

THREE - FEDERAL OPEN MARKET COMMITTEE (FOMC)

The FOMC consists of the seven members on the board of governors, plus five representatives from the regional Federal Reserve Banks (one of them is permanently from the New York Fed Bank). The FOMC is the monetary policy making body; it manipulates the flow of money and credit—primarily by setting interest rates. Formal meetings of the FOMC are typically held 8 times a year in Washington, D.C.

FOUR - FEDERAL RESERVE BANKS

There are 12 regional Federal Reserve Banks and 25 branches. Each region is independently incorporated with a 9-member board of directors from the private sector. Six are elected by member banks and three by the board of governors. They set the discount rate (Fed lending rate). However, it is subject to approval by the Board of Governors. They also watch the economy and financial institutions in their districts. Plus, they provide financial services to the United States government and depository institutions.

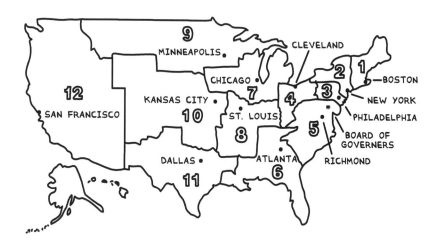

FIVE - MEMBER BANKS

The member banks are private banks. But not all private banks are member banks. There are a few different kinds of banks. There are national banks and state chartered banks. All national banks are member banks, but not all state chartered banks are member banks. Member banks elect six of the nine members of their reserve bank's board of directors. Each bank holds stock in its local Federal Reserve Bank. The stock cannot be sold or traded. Member banks receive a fixed, 6-percent dividend annually on their stock. However, the banks do not directly control their regional Federal Reserve Bank as a result of owning stock.

SIX - ADVISORY COMMITTEES

Advisory committees are used by the Federal Reserve as a means of gathering a broader array of information. Three of these committees directly advise the board of governors: the Federal Advisory Council, the Consumer Advisory Council, and the Thrift Institutions Advisory Council. Other committees advise the regional banks on matters such as agriculture and labor.

OVERVIEW

Overall, The Federal Reserve System is set up as a hierarchy of banks. Each bank owns shares in the system and the banks work together like a cartel. The biggest owners in the cartel are the biggest banks, like J.P. Morgan Chase. As will become evident in the next chapter, The Federal Reserve should be called "The Government-Supported Private Cartel of Debt Reserves."

CHAPTER SIX
WHERE DOES MONEY COME FROM?

Now that we have an understanding of the structure of the Federal Reserve System, we can look at the role the Federal Reserve plays in expanding the supply of money. Or, in other words, we can look at how the Federal Reserve magically makes new dollars.

HOW IT WORKS

It usually all starts with the Government wanting to spend more money than it takes in through taxes. And since the government doesn't ever have the fortitude to print its own money, like Lincoln did, that means it goes into debt. The government can go into debt to anyone willing to buy government treasury securities. These securities are government bonds issued by the United States Treasury; they are simply IOUs promising to pay a fixed amount of money on a fixed date in the future. Treasury securities are issued through treasury auctions. A group of banking institutions who are allowed to deal directly with the Fed, called primary dealers, buy up the majority of treasury securities for further distribution.

LIST OF THE FED'S PRIMARY DEALERS:
BNP PARIBAS, BANK OF AMERICA, BARCLAYS, CANTOR FITZGERALD, CITIGROUP, CREDIT SUISSE, DAIWA SECURITIES, DEUTSCHE BANK, GOLDMAN SACHS, RBS GREENWICH CAPITAL, HSBC SECURITIES, J. P. MORGAN, MIZUHO SECURITIES, MORGAN STANLEY, UBS SECURITIES

(2008 SAW THE LOSS OF A NUMBER OF PRIMARY DEALERS THROUGH BANKRUPTCIES AND ACQUISITIONS, LIKE, LEHMAN BROTHERS, MERRILL LYNCH, & BEAR STEARNS)

In general, when the Federal Reserve wants to add money to the system (expand the money supply), it buys treasury securities with money fabricated out of thin air. When it wants to remove money from the system (contract the money supply), it sells treasury securities. But it is able to monetize more than just treasury securities. Since the Monetary Control Act of 1980, the Fed has been able to monetize most debt instruments, including foreign debt. Consequently, the Fed can create money without getting U.S. government debt involved. But in this example, we'll concentrate on the monetization of U.S. government debt (treasury securities).

TYPES OF TREASURY SECURITIES:

TREASURY BILLS: MATURE IN LESS THAN 1 YEAR AND DON'T PAY INTEREST UNTIL MATURITY.

TREASURY NOTES: MATURE IN 2, 5, OR 10 YEARS AND ARE SOLD IN $1000 INCREMENTS. THEY PAY OUT EVERY 6 MONTHS.

TREASURY BONDS: MATURE IN 10 TO 30 YEARS. THEY PAY OUT EVERY 6 MONTHS.

TREASURY INFLATION-PROTECTED SECURITIES (TIPS): INTRODUCED IN 1997. MATURE IN 5, 7, 10, OR 20 YEARS. THE PAYOUT OF THESE IS ADJUST-ED WITH THE CONSUMER PRICE INDEX, WHICH IS AN INFLATION MEASUREMENT.

When The Federal Reserve buys treasury securities, it invents money. The Fed's money is nothing more than a bookkeeping entry (computer entry) upon which a check is written to the government by way of a primary dealer. The Federal Reserve collects interest on money it creates out of debt, but since the Federal Reserve is required to pay most of its profits to the treasury each year, the government gets what theoretically amounts to near zero interest loans from the Fed. So, the interest burden is avoided when the Federal Reserve purchases and holds treasury securities. However, only about 7% to 11% of treasury securities are held by the Fed.

The Fed records its purchased treasury securities as assets. Thus, treasury securities are used as the reserves for money creation. That is why the current system is best described as being on a debt standard.

COINS: COINS ARE THE ONLY MONEY TODAY NOT MADE FROM DEBT. COINS WERE ONCE MADE OUT OF GOLD AND SILVER BUT NOT ANYMORE. MODERN COINS ARE ESSENTIALLY DEBT-FREE MONEY, LIKE GREENBACKS AND COLONIAL SCRIP.

The newly invented money used by the Fed to purchase the treasury securities is given to the government. The government then spends the newly invented money into the system. The people who receive the new money inevitably put it into the banking system. Once the money enters the banking system, it is multiplied at least ten times through the magic of fractional reserve lending—which means that for every dollar the government borrows from the Federal Reserve, 10 or more dollars enter the system.

STEP BY STEP

Since it is a bit tricky, let us look at how all this works in more detail step by step.

ONE - DEFICIT

In typical fashion, politicians in Washington D.C. want to spend more money than they have. So, they run a deficit.

TWO - TREASURIES

Running a deficit means having the United States Treasury issue treasury securities (IOUs) to make up the deficit.

The new treasury securities are dispersed through treasury auctions. More than 800 institutions are set up to bid directly in treasury auctions. However, most bids come from primary dealers (specially selected banks and security brokers). Primary dealers are allowed to deal directly with the Federal Reserve and act as a middleman between the Fed and the government.

All kinds of entities buy up these treasury securities; they end up in the hands of governments and individuals, both domestic and foreign.

BASIC BREAKDOWN OF WHO OWNS TREASURY SECURITIES (OR, IN OTHER WORDS, WHO OWNS THE NATIONAL DEBT)

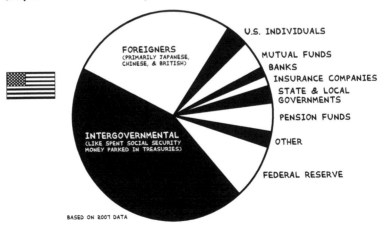

BASED ON 2007 DATA

THREE - MAGIC CHECK

When the Fed wants to add money to the system, it buys up treasury securities (or other debt instruments, like those held by banks) with imaginary money it fabricates out of thin air. When other entities (like individuals) buy treasury securities, the money to buy those already exists in the system. But the Fed's money is invented. The Fed writes a special check (enters numbers into a computer) to buy treasuries from a primary dealer. There is nothing backing this check except debt. The government's debt is the only asset upon which the money represented by the check is made. With the Fed's check, a new batch of money comes into existence—almost as if by magic.

FOUR - SPEND

The government takes this newly invented money and spends it.

FIVE - DEPOSIT

The people who get this money put it into the banking system.

SIX - BANK MONEY CREATION

Once in the banking system, through the magic of fractional reserve lending, this money is multiplied. When money is deposited into a bank checking account, the bank is required to keep 10% of that money in reserve. Interest bearing accounts, like savings accounts, require no reserves. New money deposited into the banking system becomes reserve money for making loans. When loan money is deposited into another bank, that bank can again use that same loan money to spur more lending.

Deposit money itself is not technically used as loan money in modern banking. Loan money is instead fabricated out of thin air as bookkeeping entries. The main limit on the ability of banks to create loan money is imposed by the Bank for International Settlements (the central bank of central banks) in Basel, Switzerland.

Banks must maintain total capital of at least 8% of total risk-weighted assets (loans). Total capital is the value of a bank's total assets if they were liquidated. Of that 8%, 4% must be Tier I capital. Tier I capital is the value of a bank's stock and retained earnings.

Consequently, how much money a bank can create all depends on its ability to meet capital requirements rather than simply reserve requirements.

Overall, when the Federal Reserve creates new money, the banking system ends up creating about 10 times more new money.

SEVEN - BANK INVESTING

Banks don't just lend invented money they also invest invented money. Since banks are out to maximize profits, and since demand for borrowing isn't always very high, the rules of the system allow banks to invest money. It is estimated that approximately 30% of the money created by banks is invested. Regular banks have historically invested in safe things, like treasury securities. But the repeal of the Glass Steagall act in 1999 allowed for the blending of regular, commercial banks with investment banks. Leveraged investing by banks is conducive to market manipulation, as well as upheaval (such as the market meltdown of 2008).

Maintaining this fractional reserve banking system is a balancing act. The banks need to keep up reserve and capital requirements. Everything works relatively fine as long as people pay the interest on their debt, don't try to take their money out of the bank, and don't sell bank stock—but that isn't always the case. Consequently, banks have to do things like scramble and borrow money for themselves from other banks (at the federal funds interest rate, usually overnight), or from the Fed, using the discount window.

MORE MONEY CREATION

The government isn't the only entity that borrows new money from the Fed. Banks are also allowed to borrow new money from the Fed—using the discount window. To do that, the banks need to put up collateral. The collateral they put up is debt that they hold on their books. Commercial loans are the collateral most often used. This borrowing converts old loans into new reserves. The new reserves are used to make new loans and those loans can be used as collateral for borrowing more money from the Fed. This process is commonly referred to as "discounting commercial paper."

The discount rate is on average 1% higher than the federal funds rate. Therefore, borrowing money from the Fed isn't always very appealing to banks. In response to the 2008 credit crisis, the discount rate was lowered to a mere 0.5%, while the federal funds rate went all the way down to a range of 0% to 0.25%. With that virtually free money available, many banks simply borrowed it to buy treasuries for an easy tax-payer supplied profit.

BANK RUNS

When a bank's reserves prove insufficient to meet the demand of depositors wanting to withdraw their deposits, a bank is said to become insolvent. When large amounts of people demand withdraw of their money, they quickly find out their money doesn't really exist. In U.S. banks, there are signs that say "FDIC Insured." The Federal Deposit Insurance Corporation, which was created by the Glass-Steagall Act of 1933, is a government corporation that guarantees deposits held in banks up to $100,000 per depositor. FDIC creates a moral hazard by detaching customer bank choice from risk.

 GHOST MONEY

Once you understand where money comes from in the Federal Reserve System, you realize that most money never physically exists; it is all just bookkeeping entries. Physical money only makes up a small portion of the total money supply.

Dollars in the Federal Reserve System are called "Federal Reserve Notes." A Federal Reserve Note is basically a nationalized bank note. Instead of individual banks printing up notes that say, for example, "Bank of America Note" or "Citibank Note," bank note printing is outsourced to the Bureau of Printing and Engraving and consolidated into one kind of note (The Federal Reserve Note)—which is deemed "legal tender" by the government. So, when banks need to convert their bookkeeping entries into some physical money (Federal Reserve Notes), they pay a few cents (in invented money) to have the Bureau of Engraving and Printing print it. The U.S. Mint, which was established with the Coinage Act of 1792, makes the coins. Coins are the only money form not made from debt.

 IN 2006, SPECIAL LAWS WERE IMPLEMENTED TO MAKE MELTING DOWN COINS FOR THEIR METAL CONTENT ILLEGAL. THIS WAS MADE NECESSARY BY THE FACT THAT THE VALUE OF THE METAL THAT MAKES UP PENNIES AND NICKELS WAS EXCEEDING THE FACE VALUE OF THE COINS. SUCH AN OCCURRENCE IS A COMMON, HISTORICAL SYMPTOM OF THE RAVAGES OF INFLATION.

MONEY FROM DEBT

So, that is where money comes from; it comes from debt—made by private banks through lending. The only kinds of money the federal government makes are coins and treasuries (IOUs). Regular paper dollars are created by the private banking cartel deceivingly known as the Federal Reserve.

This whole money creation scheme is weird stuff with weird implications. For instance, since the money in the Federal Reserve System is made from debt (monetizing debt), that means that if all the debt in the economy, both public and private, was paid off one day, there would be no more money left in circulation. All the money out there (except for coins) represents a debt waiting to be paid. No debt means no money.

The Federal Reserve System is fractional reserve banking on steroids. The reserves are nothing but debt (IOUs), and through leverage, that debt is multiplied into even more interest bearing debt by private banks. The great ancient, Greek scientist Archimedes once said, "Give me a place to stand, and with a lever I will move the World." The banking system operates off the same principle. "Give me a place to stand (government, with its ability to tax and make debt), and with enough leverage (fractional reserve banking) I will move the economy (inflate to put new money in the system to pay interest on old money). And that power to manipulate the economy is what centralized banking is all about; it is like a giant lever to move the economy.

CENTRALIZED BANKING

THE ECONOMY

← GOVERNMENT SANCTION

THE TAXPAYER/MONEY-USER IS THE
ULTIMATE GUARANTOR OF ALL THE DEBT,
AND THUS THE GROUND UPON WHICH IT
ALL RESTS.

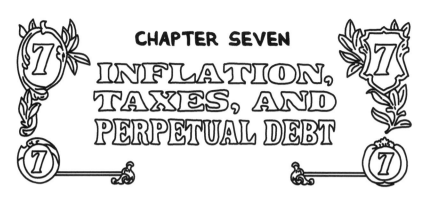

CHAPTER SEVEN
INFLATION, TAXES, AND PERPETUAL DEBT

Now that we have a good overview of where dollars come from, let's look at how politicians and banks benefit from this system at the expense of the average American citizen.

WHAT'S IN IT FOR POLITICIANS?

Obviously, the Federal Reserve System provides something of value to the politicians who operate the federal government. Otherwise, they'd campaign to get rid of it. What the Federal Reserve System gives politicians is the ability to spend more money than they bring in through taxes. Taxes are unpopular, yet people tend to vote for the politician who promises the most goodies. You can only raise taxes so much before people revolt. However, if you tax people off the record, most won't know any better. Consequently, the secret tax that the Federal Reserve System provides to politicians is inflation.

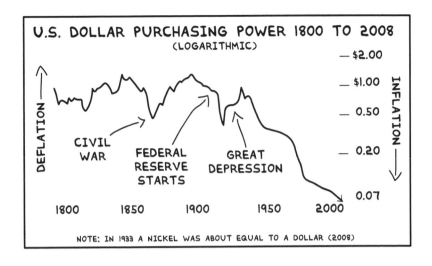

U.S. DOLLAR PURCHASING POWER 1800 TO 2008
(LOGARITHMIC)

DEFLATION →

INFLATION →

— $2.00
— $1.00
— 0.50
— 0.20
0.07

CIVIL WAR

FEDERAL RESERVE STARTS

GREAT DEPRESSION

1800   1850   1900   1950   2000

NOTE: IN 1933 A NICKEL WAS ABOUT EQUAL TO A DOLLAR (2008)

INFLATION VERSUS SUPPLY AND DEMAND

Inflation should not be confused with changes in supply and demand. Inflation is a broad increase in prices independent of particular goods and services. Conversely, supply and demand price increases are often isolated, based on a particular good or service, and are often transitory. For example, if the corn crop is bad, that means less corn. If the demand for corn stays the same, the price of corn will increase in order to tame demand to a point where supply meets demand. That kind of price increase is not really inflation; it is often isolated and often transitory. The next year corn could be a bumper crop with decreased demand—sending corn prices into a nosedive.

72

Price rises have been a recurring problem throughout history. Approximately every 200 years, there has been a big wave of price rises followed by a period of relative price stability. These price rise waves have usually corresponded with population booms and have usually ended in some variety of disaster, such as war, famine, or disease, which reduced or stabilized the population.

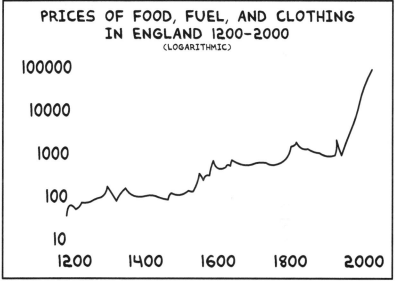

PRICES OF FOOD, FUEL, AND CLOTHING
IN ENGLAND 1200-2000
(LOGARITHMIC)

DATA BASED ON THE GREAT WAVE: PRICE REVOLUTIONS AND THE RHYTHM OF HISTORY DAVID HACKETT FISCHER

Population booms cause a number of problems involving price rises. Mainly, they mean more demand for basic goods (like grains), causing supply and demand issues. Without the proper investment to increase goods and services, prices rise.

In a sane world, with a stable population and sound money, the prices of most things would just get cheaper and cheaper. Steady productivity increases would lead to an abundant supply of goods, which, in turn, would allow people to get away with working less. Unfortunately, the world is not sane, and people sabotage their own well-being by facilitating self-defeating behaviors.

⸮ ? ⸮ MYSTERIOUS INFLATION ⸮ ? ⸮

If our money was issued directly by the government, like Lincoln's Greenbacks, it would be very obvious that the cause of inflation was government overspending (printing too much money). However, due to the middleman known as the Federal Reserve, and an ill-informed public, inflation is often treated as some kind of weird, nebulous, and unpredictable thing that just happens mysteriously. But to anyone who understands the basic workings of the system, the source of inflation is quite obvious: too much money chasing too few goods and services.

However, since money in the modern world is made out of debt, money isn't really money, it's debt. That adds another factor to the inflation equation. That factor could be described as too much debt chasing too few debt-free goods and services. If people actually had too much money, people would use it to pay off debt and clear the shelves of stores. But it is debt people have, not money.

When a bank creates $1000 as a loan at say 5% interest, the system needs an extra $50 to come into the system interest-free. Otherwise, paying the interest means more debt and interest; debt begets debt making the system dependent on an ever-increasing debt (money) supply.

There are means in the system for creating interest-free (extra) money for paying interest, such as:

PEOPLE WORKING DIRECTLY AND INDIRECTLY FOR BANKS
(BANK SPENDING)

THE FED MONETIZING GOVERNMENT DEBT

DEFAULTS ON UNSECURED DEBT
(DEBT NOT BACKED BY COLLATERAL)

TRADE SURPLUSES
(THE U.S. HAS HAD A TRADE DEFICIT SINCE THE 1960s)

However, exactly how much interest-free money can be accounted for through these means is hard to decipher. Some claim there is plenty of interest-free money to pay interest while some claim there is none. Somewhere in the middle is likely the truth.

When there is not enough interest-free money accessible in the system to pay interest, that creates a systemic struggle to make up for the missing interest money.

Those with pricing power (like businesses) can extract the missing interest money from other people by raising prices (lowering wages, outsourcing, etc.). However, those without pricing power can't; those people are left to struggle; their wages lag while prices rise, making it ever more difficult to get by without going further into debt. That leads to compounding debt and compounding interest.

WHAT IS COMPOUND INTEREST? COMPOUND INTEREST IS WHEN MONEY MADE AS INTEREST IS TURNED INTO NEW LOAN MONEY, WHICH ITSELF EARNS MORE INTEREST; THAT INTEREST IS AGAIN TURNED INTO NEW LOAN MONEY. THUS, COMPOUND INTEREST BECOMES AN EXPLOSIVE FEEDBACK LOOP THAT GROWS EXPONENTIALLY OVER TIME.

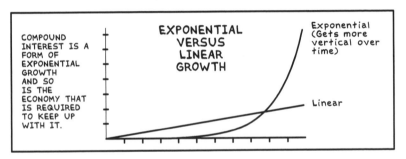

COMPOUND INTEREST IS A FORM OF EXPONENTIAL GROWTH AND SO IS THE ECONOMY THAT IS REQUIRED TO KEEP UP WITH IT.

EXPONENTIAL VERSUS LINEAR GROWTH

Exponential (Gets more vertical over time)

Linear

The elusiveness of factors like the availability of interest-free money to pay interest complicates understanding inflation. Nonetheless, inflation is ultimately a phenomenon arising from too much money (debt) chasing too few (debt-free) goods and services. The severity of debt usually corresponds with the severity of inflation (the increase in money/debt).

There is a lot of deception and misinformation that goes on in the government's reporting of inflation data—as well as other economic data, like unemployment. Inflation is essentially a hidden tax and a subsidy for banks, so underreporting inflation is an important tactic. If people got too wise to inflation, it would change their behavior and start a snowball effect of inflation evasion that would help accelerate inflation. Thus, the Federal Reserve often tries to write off inflation as mostly a psychological issue based on "inflationary expectations." However, another reason inflation is underreported is because, since things like wages and retirement benefits are adjusted according to government inflation numbers, underreporting saves the government and corporations a lot of money.

CPI AND PPI

Through the Bureau of Labor Statistics, the government measures inflation using two main indexes: the CPI and PPI.

(CPI) CONSUMER PRICE INDEX: Measures the average price of consumer goods and services.

(PPI) PRODUCER PRICE INDEX: Measures the average prices received by domestic producers for their output.

TWEAKING INFLATION NUMBERS

Here are some examples of the government's deceptive methods for underreporting inflation. These methods help keep the inflation tax hidden:

* THE CORE RATE: The "Core Rate" is the CPI or PPI excluding things like food and energy. So, there is a core CPI and a core PPI number. By excluding food and energy prices, the CPI and PPI can often be made to look lower. Therefore, although the CPI may be up 3%, the Core CPI may be unchanged.

JUST SAY NO
TO FOOD & ENERGY

* QAM: The quality adjustment method (QAM) is a means of statistical manipulation whereby price increases are written off as quality increases. So, for example, if the average price of new cars goes up 10% in one year, using the QAM, that increase can be written off saying that the new cars simply became more expensive because they got 10% better.

THE 2009 PHALLUS
XG IS NOW 10%
LONGER

* CONSUMER SUBSTITUTIONS:
If something becomes too expensive, it is assumed consumers will substitute it for something cheaper. Thus, when certain things get too expensive, they are taken out of the calculations and replaced with cheaper things.

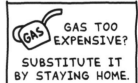

GAS TOO
EXPENSIVE?

SUBSTITUTE IT
BY STAYING HOME.

Yet, even with these kinds of statistical manipulations going on, people only need to look at their grocery bills, or something like the CRB commodities index, to see what is really going on.

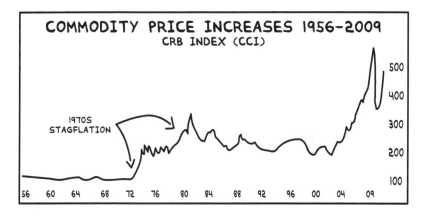

COMMODITY PRICE INCREASES 1956–2009
CRB INDEX (CCI)

1970S STAGFLATION

500
400
300
200
100

56 60 64 68 72 76 80 84 88 92 96 00 04 09

WHAT IS STAGFLATION? STAGFLATION IS INFLATION COMBINED WITH ECONOMIC STAGNATION; IT IS WHAT HAPPENS WHEN MONEY (DEBT) SUPPLY GROWS, BUT NOT THE ECONOMY.

MEASURING MONEY SUPPLY

Keeping track of how much money is out there in the system helps keep track of inflationary pressure. The money supply is quantified using four different measurements known as M0 (currency), M1, M2, and M3.

M0 (CURRENCY): The total of all physical currency, and accounts at the central bank (Fed) that can be exchanged for physical currency.

M1: M0 minus the portions of M0 held as reserves or vault cash, plus the amount in "checking" or "current" accounts.

M2: M1 plus most savings accounts, money market accounts, and certificates of deposit of under $100,000.

M3: M2 plus all other CDs, deposits of Eurodollars (overseas dollars), and repurchase agreements. (The Fed stopped reporting M3 in March of 2006.)

REPURCHASE AGREEMENT: THE FED BUYS TREASURIES (OR OTHER INSTRUMENTS, LIKE MORTGAGE-BACKED SECURITIES) FROM A PRIMARY DEALER WHO AGREES TO BUY THEM BACK (USUALLY WITHIN 1 TO 7 DAYS). THIS ALLOWS INSTITUTIONS TO TEMPORARILY TAKE THINGS LIKE TOXIC ASSETS OFF THEIR BOOKS SO THEY CAN ENGAGE IN ACCOUNTING SHENANIGANS.

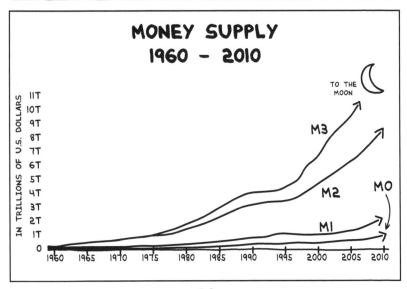

MONEY SUPPLY
1960 – 2010

VELOCITY OF MONEY

The faster money is used and reused, the more money there seems to be in existence; this is called the velocity of money. If people stopped spending money one day, it would be as if there was no money in existence. Thus, the rate of demand for and use of money helps determine the effective money supply.

SAVINGS EROSION

Since inflation erodes the purchasing power of dollars and drives up costs, it makes past debts less significant. So, anyone who saves money is robbed by inflation. That means that savings must be put to work to beat inflation. But putting money to work increases the velocity of money, which expands the effective money supply. That is itself potentially inflationary. On top of all that, gains on investments are subject to taxes. So, that money has to be made up too. Consequently, trying to beat inflation is often a lot like climbing a perpetually ascending staircase—at best, you just end up back where you started no matter how hard you try.

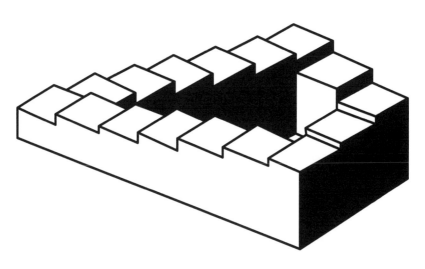

 INCOME TAX

The Tariff Act of October 3, 1913, brought federal income tax to the United States. A few months later, the Federal Reserve Act was passed. Unfortunately, most Americans don't even realize that prior to 1913, there was no such thing as income tax. Taxes on income were tried from time to time prior to 1913, but when put to the test (courts), the idea of income tax was considered un-constitutional. Income tax is a direct tax in contradiction of Article I, section 9, of the U.S. Constitution, which states that "No capitation, or other direct, tax shall be laid, unless in proportion to the census or enumeration herein before directed to be taken." In other words, income can't be taxed unless everyone pays an equal por-tion.

At first, income tax didn't apply to most people and so most people didn't think much of it. In 1914, income tax rates were modest, only 1% (up to $20,000) for the bottom bracket and 7% for the top bracket (over $500,000). But the tax rates steadily rose as debt rose. And the complexity of the tax system also rose in order to build loopholes and support a growing industry of tax preparation professionals. The 1940s and World War II brought a huge spike in income taxes that lasted into the early 1960s; the tax brackets went as high as 94% for the top bracket and as high as 23% for the bottom bracket. Into the 1980s, the top bracket was still around 70% for income over $100,000.

SOCIAL SECURITY: IN THE MID 1930S, A NEW TAX WAS ADDED ONTO THE INCOME TAX CALLED SOCIAL SECURITY. SOCIAL SECURITY IS USED BY POLITICIANS TO HOLD DEBT. EACH YEAR, SURPLUS MONEY PAID INTO SOCIAL SECURITY IS SPENT AND TURNED INTO GOVERNMENT DEBT. SINCE THE GOVERNMENT DEBT THAT THIS MONEY IS TURNED INTO EARNS INTEREST, SOCIAL SECURITY IS ADVERTISED AS A MEANS OF SAFELY SAVING MONEY FOR RETIREMENT. HOWEVER, IT IS IN MANY WAYS SIMPLY ANOTHER SOURCE OF TAX MONEY FOR THE GOVERNMENT TO SPEND. AND INEVITABLY, IT IS AN UNSUSTAINABLE PYRAMID SCHEME REQUIRING EVER GREATER PARTICIPANTS AND OR PAYMENTS.

Taxpayers/money-users are the ultimate guarantors of the Federal Reserve System. So, the federal government's ability to tax is important. People with higher incomes pay a higher percentage of their money to taxes like federal income tax. People with lower incomes pay a higher percentage of their money to taxes like sales tax and the hidden tax of inflation. When all types of taxes are added together, most Americans work over one-third of the year just to pay taxes. Some of those taxes (mostly local taxes) go to things people actually care about. However, most taxes (especially federal taxes) simply go to big government, war, and servicing debt.

The whole point of implementing the income tax in 1913 (in conjunction with starting the Federal Reserve System) was to secure a source of revenue for the government to keep the interest on its future debt paid. If the country controlled its spending and issued its own money debt-free, there would be no need for an income tax.

THE NATIONAL DEBT

Interest on the national debt has grown to costing Americans around a half a trillion dollars a year (it is becoming unsustainable). The national debt in 1913 was just under 3 billion dollars. By 1919, it was over 27 billion. The roaring twenties saw debt shrink, even as money supply expanded (this was due to the use of commercial bank loans as reserves by the Fed to expand the money supply). However, debt rose again during the Great Depression. By the end of World War II, the national debt was over 250 billion. In 1981, it hit 1 trillion. And in 2008, it reached the 10 trillion mark.

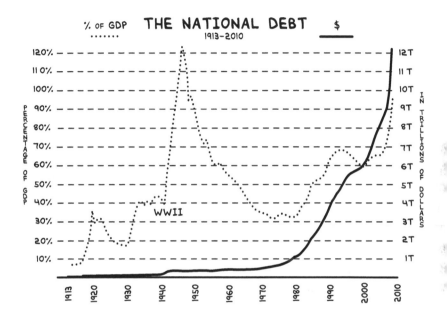

THE NATIONAL DEBT
% OF GDP ....   1913-2010 $ ——

GDP: GDP IS THE GROSS DOMESTIC PRODUCT. GDP IS THE TOTAL MARKET VALUE OF ALL FINAL GOODS AND SERVICES PRODUCED WITHIN A COUNTRY IN A GIVEN TIME PERIOD.

GDP = CONSUMPTION + GROSS INVESTMENT + GOVERNMENT SPENDING + (EXPORTS - IMPORTS).

NOTE: THE WAY MODERN GDP IS CALCULATED IS RIDICULOUS SINCE IT COUNTS CONSUMPTION (WHICH IS OFTEN FUELED BY DEBT) AND GOVERNMENT DEBT ACCUMULATION AS ECONOMIC GROWTH.

VISUALIZING THE DEBT

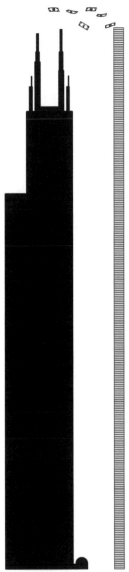

A stack of $100 bills equaling 1 million dollars stands about 40 inches. That means a stack the size of the Sears Tower would equal about 435 million dollars. To equal 1 Trillion dollars, you would need about 2,300 Sears Tower high stacks. The national debt is more than 10 Trillion dollars. That means that a stack of $100 bills equaling the size of the national debt would extend over 6000 miles into space.

$435
MILLION

$10
TRILLION

$100
BILLS
(STACKED)
HEIGHT
6,310 MILES

SEARS
TOWER
(CHICAGO)
HEIGHT
1,451 FEET

$100
BILLS
(STACKED)
HEIGHT
1,451 FEET

EARTH
DIAMETER
7,926 MILES

NO DEBT = NO MONEY

It is pointless to talk about paying down the national debt without monetary reform. There is no escaping debt in the Federal Reserve System; no debt means no money. The debt can exist in many forms, not just national debt. However, since private debt is paid off at a steady pace, that money is cycled out of existence. The only debt that reliably grows without ever being paid off is the national debt; merely the interest is ever paid.

Since debt means interest, debt money is parasitic; it either feeds on people's labor and productivity, or it simply requires more debt to be maintained. When debt growth contracts, effective and or real money supply contracts—as happened with the 2008 credit crisis. That is what leads to deflation. Within the Federal Reserve System, the solution to such a crisis rests in getting the debt expanding again—namely through national debt. At a certain point though, you just can't keep making debt, because the interest burden becomes too great. The interest compounds, which is a form of exponential growth. Exponential interest growth requires exponential money supply growth (Fed monetization of debt), and eventually the economy just can't keep up and grow in tandem with money supply growth. Growing money supply without corresponding economic growth to increase goods and services means inflation. On the other hand, insufficient money supply growth means deflation.

FIRST SPENDER

When the supply of money is increased in the normal way, through debt purchased by the Federal Reserve with newly invented dollars, inflation (eroded purchasing power) doesn't start until after that money is spent. So, whoever spends the money first gets the full benefit of the new money. If the new money is spent wisely, it grows the economy in proportion with itself. However, new money usually isn't spent wisely; it often comes into existence simply to pay what amounts to interest on old money and to consume.

Not all money (debt) is spent domestically, especially since oil is still traded internationally in dollars. Thus, a large percentage of dollars go overseas. That mutes inflation, but exporting dollars only works for as long as people want them. As the stability and soundness of the dollar comes into question, the ability to export dollars will become more difficult. Inevitably, people will want to spend those dollars back to America. That is what would be called inflation coming home to roost.

Since the government is often the first spender of new money, it gets the most benefit. The second spender is whoever gets the money from the government first—or whoever borrows the money from the Federal Reserve and the banks first. Due to inflation, the ability to save enough money to buy things without going into debt is ever more difficult. And that increases demand for borrowing. Inflation benefits borrowers because it makes past debts worth less. However, borrowing requires paying interest. So, the bankers are really the winners of borrowing; the inflation gain of borrowing is surrendered to the banks through interest.

BUBBLE MACHINE

New money often helps create asset bubbles (instead of useful economic activity). Those who get the new money first start the bubbles. Thus, they profit from the bubbles the most. The people who get in last end up paying for the profits provided to the people who got in first. Bubbles are the part of inflation that people tend to like. People like it when their houses or stock portfolios are increasing in value.

While in theory the Federal Reserve is supposed to prevent things like bubbles, it is actually the leading engine for facilitating bubbles. That is because the Fed maintains the bubble of all bubbles, which is the credit bubble (mainly, by keeping interest rates artificially low).

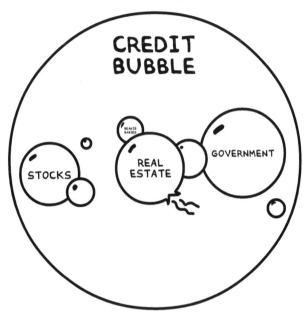

In general, the 80s and 90s saw money flood into paper assets, like stocks. And the dot com bubble of the late 90s, which epitomized that era's "irrational exuberance" for speculating in paper assets, ushered in the climax of that trend. After the dot com bubble burst, the new big bubble became real estate. Extra low interest rates and loose lending facilitated a frenzy in real estate speculation. In certain hot locations, home prices doubled in just a few years.

MEDIAN U.S. HOUSE PRICES
1963-2008
(IN THOUSANDS OF DOLLARS)

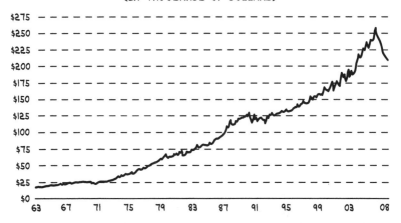

FINANCING
BUBBLY CONSUMPTION

IN THE LAST FEW DECADES, AMERICA HAS BECOME A
DEBTOR NATION AS OPPOSED TO A CREDITOR NATION.
AND AMERICA'S PREMIER CREDITOR HAS BECOME CHINA.
ALTHOUGH THE CHINESE MAKE A LOT LESS MONEY THAN
AMERICANS DO, THEY ACTUALLY SAVE THEIR MONEY.
CHINESE SAVE NEARLY HALF THEIR MONEY WHILE AMER-
ICANS SAVE NEARLY NONE. FURTHERMORE, CHINA AC-
TUALLY PRODUCES TANGIBLE GOODS WHILE AMERICA'S
ECONOMY HAS BECOME A PHONY SERVICE ECONOMY BASED
ON CONSUMPTION.

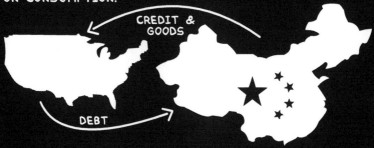

CHINESE CREDIT HELPED FUEL THE U.S. HOUSING
BUBBLE, WHICH PEAKED IN 2006.

PROFITING FROM REAL ESTATE

Real estate is a hard asset, and longer term it tends to work as a hedge against inflation. There are a lot of expenses that go into owning a home, and many of those expenses simply increase as the home's value increases (like property taxes and insurance). Nonetheless, the biggest expense for most homeowners is the mortgage. Since home prices tend to get ever higher, ever less people are able to buy a home without borrowing money. But the real estate market depends on the availability of bank loans. When banks stop lending, the real estate market dries up.

HERE ARE SOME EXAMPLES OF HOW MUCH A BANK STANDS TO MAKE OFF A LOAN FOR $200,000 TO BUY A HOUSE:

* $200,000 LOAN FOR 30 YEARS AT 7% = $479,016
  BANK REVENUE IS $279,016

* $200,000 LOAN FOR 30 YEARS AT 5% = $386,510
  BANK REVENUE IS $186,510

* $200,000 LOAN FOR 20 YEARS AT 7% = $372,144
  BANK REVENUE IS $172,144

Only part of the money used to buy a house is profit for the people who actually labored away to build the house. Therefore, the bank stands to make much more money off a house's sale than the people who actually built the house. That wouldn't be so unfair if the money borrowed to buy the house was legit. But when you consider that the bank, for the most part, simply loans invented money made through fractional reserve lending, it is a big scam. Don't you wish you could lend people imaginary money at interest?

Before a mortgage is all paid off, real estate prices often appreciate enough to make up for the money lost to interest. But if your house went up in value, that probably means most other houses did too. So, selling your house and buying a new one won't often do you much good, unless you move to a location with a depressed real estate market. At best, owning a home for most people is only beneficial in the sense that it is a store of saved money that may have otherwise not been saved. Real profit in real estate usually only comes when you own multiple properties with minimal or no debt.

(MBS) MORTGAGE BACKED SECURITIES: IN RECENT YEARS, BANKS HAVE ADDED AN EXTRA LAYER OF PRECARIOUS ABSTRACTION TO LOANING MONEY BY PACKAGING LARGE BLOCKS OF LOANS AND SELLING THEM OFF AS MORTGAGE BACKED SECURITIES. SELLING OFF LOANS ALLOWS BANKS TO MAKE MORE LOANS AND MAKE RISKIER LOANS. TO MAKE SELLING OFF LOANS MORE APPEALING TO INVESTORS, SELLERS OFFER DERIVATIVES KNOWN AS CREDIT DEFAULT SWAPS AS INSURANCE AGAINST PEOPLE DEFAULTING ON THEIR DEBT.

DERIVATIVES

The housing bubble that peaked in 2006 was driven in large part by loose lending facilitated and justified by financial instruments known as derivatives. Derivatives are basically instruments for betting on the future value of an asset. They require little (or even no) money down, and they are often used as a kind of insurance for managing and off-loading risk. Derivatives are a symptom of the kind of abstract insanity used to further expand credit in an already severely over extended system. The value of all the derivatives in existence is estimated at hundreds of trillions of dollars—a value far exceeding the amount of actual money in existence.

In his annual letter to shareholders, in 2002, billionaire Warren Buffet called derivatives "financial weapons of mass destruction carrying dangers that, while now latent, are potentially lethal." Derivatives are not much different than bets placed with a bookie. The bets are technically unfunded, shrouded in privacy, and ungrounded in things like actual businesses making money by providing actual goods and services. All that matters is that the bets pay off—even if the bets are on disaster.

BAILOUTS

Although banks have a lot of money at their disposal, it is still all a very precarious venture. That is because it is all so highly leveraged and abstract. When that leverage and abstraction gets out of hand and causes problems, the Federal Reserve System allows for bailouts. Bailouts are used in an effort to avoid a cascade effect. That means that the average American taxpayer is the guarantor of last resort on all the debt in the system. Any big entity, whether a bank or a corporation tied into banking interests, in need of a liquidity injection, has access to one by way of the Federal Reserve.

The little guys aren't all that important, only the big guys (that is, unless a bunch of little guys have the big guys in a bind). The little guys are the competition of the big guys. The big guys have the advantage of being too big to let fail. That means, since failure could noticeably hurt the economy, bail out is justified. And too big to let fail also sometimes means bailing out foreign governments. The bailouts are usually structured so that the government (taxpayers) has a theoretical possibility of, in the end, profiting from taking on the risk inherent in the bailout plan. But realistically, if the profit potential was really so high, private investors would go in and bail out the struggling institution.

Ultimately, due to government complacency in supporting inept and problematic institutions, bailouts act as an enabler of excessive risk taking and general inefficiency. Being too big to let fail means things that should be left to bankruptcy and cleansed from the system aren't. Plus, it is a recipe for making institutions that eventually become too big to even bail.

SOME EXAMPLES OF BAILOUTS

MORTGAGE BAILOUT
1933
(FORMED THE HOME OWNERS' LOAN CORP)

THE PENN CENTRAL RAILROAD
1970

LOCKHEED
1971

NEW YORK CITY
1975

CHRYSLER
1978

SAVINGS AND
LOAN CRISIS
1989

MEXICO
1995

LONG-TERM
CAPITAL
MANAGEMENT
1998

THE AIRLINE INDUSTRY
2001

THE 2008 MEGA BAILOUTS

THE BIG, BAD MORTGAGE BAILOUTS

(FANNIE MAE, & FREDDIE MAC WERE LEVERAGED AS MUCH AS 150 TO 1)

(INVESTMENT BANKS WERE LEVERAGED AS MUCH AS 40 TO 1)

BEAR STEARNS

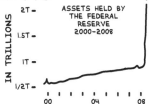

ASSETS HELD BY THE FEDERAL RESERVE 2000-2008

QUANTITATIVE EASING

IN RESPONSE TO THE 2008 CREDIT CRISES, THE FEDERAL RESERVE CREATED TRILLIONS OF DOLLARS IN NEW MONEY.

EMERGENCY ECONOMIC STABILIZATION ACT

IN 2008, LEGISLATION WAS PASSED AUTHORIZING THE SECRETARY OF THE TREASURY TO SPEND UP TO $700 BILLION TO PURCHASE DISTRESSED ASSETS FROM THE NATION'S BANKS (LIKE MORTGAGE-BACKED SECURITIES), AND TO INJECT CAPITAL INTO BANKS.

MARK-TO-MARKET ACCOUNTING

A RULE CHANGE ELIMINATING MARK-TO-MARKET ACCOUNTING (ASSIGNING A VALUE TO A POSITION HELD IN A FINANCIAL INSTRUMENT BASED ON THE CURRENT FAIR MARKET PRICE) HELPED TURN THE STOCK MARKET AROUND IN MARCH OF 2009. THIS ELIMINATED THE REPORTING OF LARGE LOSSES BY COMPANIES HOLDING DISTRESSED ASSETS.

 LET IT BURN!

As long as a money system makes money out of debt, the economy facilitated by that money system will want to boom and bust. In such a system (like the present system), busts are good, healthy things; they are like forest fires; they clear away the dead weight in the economy (the stuff that is simply surviving on credit instead of efficiently producing something valuable). The more frequently busts occur, the lighter, quicker, and more dispersed they are. However, governments (and people in general) tend to want to prevent busts. The result is similar to Smokey the Bear wanting to prevent forest fires.

Preventing busts causes the economy to become way over-extended and filled with toxic fuel that simply makes the inevitable bust huge and prolonged. What's worse is that the modern economy is very much integrated and synchronized. When the busts come, they spread like wildfire. That is when governments (fire fighters) come in and try to stop the busts. But the fact is, booms need to bust. When busting is prevented for too long, the system reaches a point where there is just so much fuel for the fire that trying to extinguish the impending bust only prolongs the bust (turning it into a slow burn).

ONLY FOOLS DELAY BUSTS.

THE BUST PREVENTION SQUAD

GOVERNMENT: MAKE DEBT (THE MONEY SUPPLY) BIGGER THROUGH INCREASED SPENDING.

FEDERAL RESERVE: MAKE INTEREST RATES ARTIFICIALLY LOW TO SPUR EVER MORE BORROWING TO PREVENT DEFAULTS.

FINANCIAL INSTITUTIONS: MAKE CHANGES IN ACCOUNTING METHODS AND MAKE TOOLS LIKE DERIVATIVES TO HIDE AND DIVERT LOSSES.

WINNERS & LOSERS
IN THE FEDERAL RESERVE SYSTEM

WINNERS

BANKS: Banks are allowed to practice fractional reserve lending, which gives them a monopoly on creating money. Banks get to borrow money from the Fed's discount window, loan out invented money, and profit off making nothing that is real. So, they don't have much to lose and a lot to gain. As long as there is inflation, there will be enough money in the system to collect interest and make new loans. And even if the scam falls apart (which is bound to happen), it is no big deal. If the government won't bail out the bank, it will at least bail out depositors.

MOOCHERS: Those who get money from the government capitalize off the government's ability to make debt. Moochers come in many forms. However, the corporate moochers, like the Industrial Military Complex, are the most notable.

RISK DIVERTING MOOCHERS: There are people who borrow money parasitically to turn a big, leveraged profit. If the venture fails, bankruptcy saves them.

GOVERNMENT: The system allows the government to take out what amount to interest-free loans so it can spend money it doesn't have. Additionally, any profits off interest the Fed makes from lending banks money is refunded to the government. That allows both banks and the government to profit off interest in a symbiotic relationship. In addition, the inflation caused by making ever more money to pay ever more debt makes the government's past debts worth ever less by devaluing the dollar. People with saved money need to invest it to keep up with inflation. Gains on those investments, even if they fall short of keeping up with inflation, are taxed. That provides even more money to the government.

LOSERS

GOVERNMENT: Although the government wins in a number of ways in the Federal Reserve System, the government is only a winner in the sense that it is in cahoots with the private banking system. Realistically, the government would be a much bigger winner if it took back its ability to issue the nation's money. In such a scenario, the citizens could actually be winners in conjunction with the government. The debt burden would be gone and so would the need for most taxation. When the government works for private banking interests, the people lose and banks win.

BORROWERS: Most borrowers lose more to interest than they gain from inflation. In addition, if a borrower defaults on something like a house, then that person can lose the house (plus the money paid into it). If a person like that tried to file bankruptcy, that person could be subject to things like garnished wages.

SAVERS AND TAXPAYERS: Inflation dissolves away the value of savings. So, savers are forced to put their money to work to make some capital gains. But capital gains are taxed. Taxes along with inflation pay for the system to the benefit of the winners in the system.

WORKERS: Pay almost always lags behind inflation.

THE RESULTS

1) An unproductive private banking and finance industry with huge, parasitic profits.

2) A big, incompetent, money-dictated government becoming ever more indebted.

3) An indebted middle class with negative savings.

CORPORATIST NATION

The country is run by money. That wouldn't be so much of a problem if the government—working for the people—had control of the money (or the people had control of the money). However, the private banking cartel, headed by the Federal Reserve, issues the country's money. Nearly all the dollars in existence were created by the banks through loans. Day in and day out the banks collect interest on those dollars. Consequently, the banks run the money and thus run the country. That kind of set up is what is called corporatism (or a plutocracy). Corporatism gives both capitalism and government a bad name because it disguises itself as capitalism and government while working on behalf of its own interests. There is hardly a more lucrative scheme than to make money out of debt; it means that the more wealth a nation creates the more debt it creates. Thus, banks get paid for wealth creation by taking wealth from the people who actually created the wealth. As a result, the top one percent of the U.S. population controls more financial wealth than the bottom 95 percent.

THIS NOTE IS LEGAL TENDER
FOR ALL DEBTS, PUBLIC AND PRIVATE

CHAPTER EIGHT

BETTER MONEY

Now that we know what is going on with our money today, it is time to figure out what we should do about it.

There are three main views concerning America's money. Those three main views are Debt, Gold, and Government Paper. The debt view essentially defends the current system. The gold view defends the definition of money in the Constitution. And the government paper view defends the stance that the government should just print its own debt-free, fiat money—like Lincoln and the colonies did. We've already covered the debt view of money embodied by the Federal Reserve System. Now we need to look at the potential of gold and government paper to save us from the current system.

 NEW GOLD

Implementing a gold or silver backed currency in the contemporary world is a questionable objective. Where do you get the gold or silver from? How do you pay for it? And how much is there? Is there really enough to make it a viable backing for money?

The fact is, gold and other precious metals already are money today. The only problem is that, through taxation, government hinders gold's interchangeability with dollars.

The easiest thing the government could do to respect the "real money" status of gold and silver—as defined in the U.S. Constitution—would be to make precious metals tax-free. That way, precious metals would be seamlessly exchangeable for dollars. Hence, they'd be like regular money. And they'd act as a simple alternative to dollars for people wanting to hedge against inflation.

A bill to end taxes on precious metals was actually proposed to congress February 13, 2008, by Texas Congressman Ron Paul. The bill was called the "Tax-Free Gold Act of 2008." The bill didn't go anywhere though. Most people in congress don't understand much, let alone money.

NEW GOVERNMENT PAPER

The government is trillions of dollars in debt and the government pays interest on that debt. That is mind-bogglingly stupid when you consider that the government could just print its own money debt-free. The classic issue cited with letting the government print its own money is that it is a recipe for potentially high inflation. However, that all depends on how it is done. The economy could absorb any amount of new money as long as that money was interest-free and used to increase

105

goods and services. Printing money isn't the problem in as much as borrowing money is the problem. Borrowing means interest. Interest is a parasite on a money supply; it forces a money supply to want to grow simply to prevent defaults on debt. When a government is enticed into debt by its very money system, as happens in the current system, it has a bias of wanting to inflate. If the government can issue an IOU in the form of a treasury security, it can print money.

 # TRILLION DOLLAR COIN

The government can and does make coins, so even if it is afraid to print its own paper money, it could always issue large denomination coins. Realistically, if the government wanted to pay the national debt off one day, it could just make some fancy million, billion, or even trillion dollar coins as payment. That would save the country from the annual national debt interest bill, which has grown to being nearly a half a trillion dollars a year. Plus, since treasuries are treated in many ways like regular money, the coins would just cancel out that existing debt/money, which would mean the coins wouldn't even necessarily be very inflationary.

INFRASTRUCTURE DOLLARS

There is nothing wrong with the government making its own money; it just has to do it properly and with limitation. Consequently, if the government started printing its own debt-free money, precise rules would have to be established in order for it to be done right. One of the best ideas for implementing a sound form of government paper money is an idea reminiscent of Jacob Coxey's greenbacks for infrastructure idea of the 1890s. In such a system, new money would enter the economy only when the government spent new money on building and maintaining infrastructure. So, for example, infrastructure, like transportation systems (bridges, roads, rails), would be funded and backed by debt-free paper money.

There would be a number of benefits to such a system. Mainly, it would mean being able to build and maintain infrastructure that is conducive to a healthy economy without debt or taxation. Plus, having money backed by a hard asset like infrastructure would make the system somewhat similar to gold or silver backed money. There would be real labor behind the money and real assets.

The fact is, the government does and will continue to spend money on needed infrastructure one way or another regardless of the means. With infrastructure dollars, it would get to do so without debt (interest) and without taxation.

HOW INFRASTRUCTURE DOLLARS WOULD WORK

FIND OUT WHAT NEEDS BUILT.

IN THE SAME WAY THEY DECIDE TODAY, STATES AND LOCAL GOVERNMENTS WOULD DECIDE WHAT INFRASTRUCTURE THEY NEED.

FIND OUT IF LABOR AND MATERIALS ARE AVAILABLE.

IF LABOR AND MATERIALS ARE AVAILABLE, THAT PROBABLY MEANS THE ECONOMY IS NOT AWASH IN TOO MUCH MONEY. THUS, PRINTING NEW INFRASTRUCTURE DOLLARS WOULD BE JUSTIFIABLE.

PRINT NEW MONEY.

PAY THE WORKERS AND MATERIALS SUPPLIERS WHO CONSTRUCT THE PROJECT WITH THE NEW MONEY.

EACH PROJECT COSTING OVER A CERTAIN AMOUNT OF MONEY WOULD GET SPECIALLY DESIGNED BILLS DEPICTING THE PROJECT BACKING THE BILLS. EACH BILL WOULD BE INDIVIDUALLY MARKED WITH A NUMBER CORRESPONDING WITH A PUBLICLY ACCESSIBLE RECEIPT. ALL EXPENSES WOULD BE PAID USING INDIVIDUALLY MARKED, PHYSICAL BILLS (NOT DIGITAL BILLS).

THE RECIPIENTS SPEND THE NEW MONEY INTO THE REST OF THE ECONOMY.

HONEST BANKS

If the government started printing its own debt-free money (like through infrastructure dollars), the full benefits of such a setup wouldn't transpire unless banks were reformed. Otherwise, banks would perpetuate the current inflationary system by further expanding the debt supply through fractional reserve lending.

Just because it is legal under a debt monetary system for a bank to lend out more money than it has in reserves doesn't mean it is honest. An honest bank would primarily make money by charging service fees. An honest bank wouldn't make loans with invented money. With an honest bank, money deposited in the bank would stay in the bank—unless the depositor explicitly agreed otherwise.

There are a few historical examples of honest banks, starting with The Bank of Venice and ending with The Bank of Hamburg; in between the two was The Bank of

Amsterdam. Honest banks, by being honest, facilitate honest economies. They don't suffer from the disease of leverage and predatory interest that comes when money is fabricated out of fractional reserves.

NO LEGAL TENDER
NO FRACTIONAL RESERVE LENDING

Although people are socially conditioned to think of money in association with the government and banks, there is nothing that says the government and banks need to be involved with money. If people were unrestricted by legal tender laws and taxation, then people would be free to accept whatever they want as money. And without the unfair advantage of banks being permitted to use fractional reserve lending to lend invented money, people with savings would be the lenders in society. Things such as websites where individuals loan out chunks of money (diversified lending) and people borrow chunks of money (diversified borrowing) would be competitive banks.

BRINGING IT ALL TOGETHER

To make the change over to new money, people would first need to elect competent, knowledgeable, and honest politicians to various levels of government. However, the only hope of getting those kinds of politicians would be if voters suddenly became a lot smarter. As it stands, even something as simple as "tax-free gold" has very little public understanding or congressional support.

Tax-free gold could be very easily implemented, and it would make a great start to changing over to debt-free money. Next, the government would need to take back its ability to create money. That could be done with infrastructure dollars. Infrastructure dollars could first be implemented by individual states by starting state owned banks. Those banks could thus create interest-free credit for infrastructure projects. That is actually done to some extent today in the state of North Dakota.

Once implemented at the state level, the federal government could do the same and thus make infrastructure dollars national. By harnessing the power to create money, the government would need progressively less taxation. That would lead to numerous tax-free hard assets—other than just precious metals. Tax-free hard assets would create healthy competition with the dollar. Legal tender status could be switched over from debt dollars to infrastructure dollars. Infrastructure dollars would eliminate the need for government debt and eliminate most taxation—from the federal level to the local level.

Seeing as the new infrastructure money would be debt-free (and thus interest-free), the old debt system would need phased out. Otherwise, regular banks would still control the issuance of most of the nation's money through fractional reserve lending. The Federal Reserve's new job would be the dismantling of the Federal Reserve System. That would require taxing the interest on debt that was monetized back in the old system. Otherwise, the money made by the new system would simply get sucked back up paying off interest from the old system. Revenues from this tax would be used to smooth the transition for citizens detrimentally impacted by the change over to the new system. Additionally, reserve requirements for banks would be incrementally raised until fractional reserve banking was eliminated and replaced by honest banking. The lack of private bank credit would be made up by the ample savings of the American people.

In the end, infrastructure dollars would marry debt-free paper money with a non-finite hard asset (infrastructure) while eliminating the need for most taxation. All the government would have to do is take back its power to create money from the banking system.

It is really pretty simple stuff. What isn't simple is the complex web of insanity that it would eliminate.

THE RESULTS OF
INFRASTRUCTURE DOLLARS

* The U.S. would have amazing infrastructure. Also, since that infrastructure would be the backing of the dollar, the dollar would be an extremely desirable currency.

* America would shine as a beacon over the rest of the world still mired in the old, parasitic debt monetary system.

* There would be a lot of work available. Freedom from taxation, inflation, and debt dependence would free up capital and mean people would retain most of the value of their labors. In addition, if people really wanted something like government health insurance, the country could actually afford it. But most people would have plenty of money. So, things like paying for healthcare would likely not be issues for most people.

* New money would come into the system in a manner that assists commerce and runs proportionate to growth (and or sustainability). No one would get any infrastructure money until the required work to back the money was done. That is counter-inflationary. In addition, since government money would be competing directly with other forms of money, like gold, inflation would be kept under control.

* Financial institutions would be honest by keeping full reserves. So, insolvency would not be an issue. The leveraged, parasitic aspects of the debt monetary system would be gone. Individuals with savings would, through tools like lending websites,

become competitive lenders deciding who gets money.

* People could actually plan for retirement without worrying about their savings being stolen through inflation.

* Government would shrink because people would be ever less dependent on its assistance for anything except money creation trough infrastructure construction.

* The government would not be allowed to print money to pay for the military in the new system. That means that if the American people wanted something like war, they'd have to pay for it directly through special, temporary taxation. Consequently, peace would be highly preferred. You would see the military serving the economical and peaceful role of simple homeland defense, as opposed to international entanglement and aggression. The debt dependent excesses of the industrial military complex would be a relic of the past.

* Infrastructure dollars would likely be implemented by other countries and perhaps become the international standard of money creation.

* Overall, we would no longer have the government-manipulated, corporatist, corrupt, debt-ridden, inflationary, poor excuse for a free, capitalist economy that we have today. Nor would we have the lame, debt-facilitated, corporatist attempts at socialism. Instead, we would have the best of capitalism combined only with the best of what government has to offer socially.

WOULDN'T IT BE NICE?

   While better money would be great, going beyond money would be even greater. The ultimate goal of economic activity should be economic transcendence. That could be accomplished through the construction of a small device that reprograms subatomic particles, and runs on effectively infinite, free energy (like zero-point quantum vacuum energy). With such a device, a person could, for instance, turn some dirt into an apple, or a mansion. Once one of these devices was made, it would be able to replicate itself. With such a device, the world would be like a virtual reality without scarcity; it would mean the end of economics and the end of the need for money.

CHAPTER NINE
AVERTING DISASTER

If the nation had competent, uncorrupted leaders and knowledgeable citizenry, any cracks in the system would be immediately seized as the perfect opportunity to make the move over to debt-free money. However, until the nation becomes knowledgeable about the true nature of its money, it will remain ignorantly enslaved to the ever-magnified deficiencies of the debt system.

The system is based on perpetual debt, which, since the money to maintain that debt theoretically comes from growth and productivity, requires perpetual growth and productivity. But no amount of growth and productivity actually makes new money. The money needed to pay interest on existing debt requires more money and debt (or working directly for the creditor). So, thanks to the compounding of interest, the system creates a kind of accelerating treadmill economy of perpetual debt requiring exponential growth. Unless growth keeps up to absorb the new money entering the system, the result is inflation.

THE REAL ENVIRONMENTAL PROBLEM IS DEBT-BASED MONEY

SINCE THE CURRENT ECONOMY IS DEPENDENT ON PERPETUAL DEBT AND PERPETUAL GROWTH, IT MUST PERPETUALLY AND EXPONENTIALLY CONSUME RESOURCES. IN OTHER WORDS, IT IS UNSUSTAINABLE. ENVIRONMENTALISM IS A LOSING BATTLE UNTIL THERE ARE FUNDAMENTAL CHANGES IN THE NATURE OF MONEY.

Perpetual debt means passing on ever-greater amounts of debt to future generations. But eventually, that burden will just be too much to bear. Although the current national debt is around 12 trillion dollars, that doesn't include things like all the future government promises made through entitlement programs, such as Social Security and Medicare. When you add those future promises to the existing debt, the total number comes out to as much as 100 trillion dollars.

The pyramid scheme known as social security is beginning to pay out more money than it takes in. For many years, surpluses in social security have been spent by the government to make up for overspending. So, that is a problem. Other unfunded government retirement programs, like government employee programs, are also problems. However, the really big problem is the expense of unfunded Medicare promises. Therefore, something's going to have to give. There really are no free lunches—unless perhaps if you die before the bill comes. The old inflation scheme blows up when, instead of trying to erase past debt, the government makes promises about future debt.

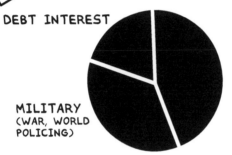

WHERE FEDERAL TAX MONEY GOES IN AN AVERAGE YEAR

DEBT INTEREST

OTHER
(MISCELLANEOUS BUREAUCRACY, MEDICARE, MEDICAID, CORPORATE WELFARE, ETC.)

MILITARY
(WAR, WORLD POLICING)

Most people don't realize that programs like Social Security and Medicare exist precisely because our debt monetary system robs people of so much of their wealth. If people kept the full value of their labor and weren't robbed by interest, inflation, and taxation, they'd have plenty of money for healthcare and retirement. Thus, they'd be free from employer healthcare and retirement serfdom.

When you consider the fact that most people spend their days toiling away at creating value, it seems pretty ridiculous that there should be so much debt. Where's all that value going? Well, since the monetary system is so parasitic, that value is transferred to the masters of the debt system. And those masters use that money to do things like control education and media in order to direct the public discourse in their favor. The surface motives vary, but the underlying motive of keeping the debt system rolling is shared by all the debt masters. The question is though, how much longer can they keep the public asleep?

The government's debt is just a reflection of the much larger private debt permeating the system, and the system is breaking; it is breaking in the sense that it is beyond any sort of a quick fix. Because, as the old saying goes, you can't squeeze blood from a turnip. The debt is becoming too big to maintain. Perhaps we could luck out and discover some magic bean to keep the game going a little while longer. However, in the end, there are really only two options: excessive inflation (perhaps even hyperinflation) and or major depression. Excessive inflation means devaluing the dollar to wipe out old debts, while depression means defaulting on debts.

WHAT IS HYPERINFLATION? WHEN INFLATION BECOMES EXTREME, IT BECOMES HYPERINFLATION. WITH HYPERINFLATION, THE PURCHASING POWER OF A PAPER CURRENCY RAPIDLY DISSOLVES. THERE ARE NUMEROUS EXAMPLES OF HYPERINFLATION, SUCH AS GERMANY (WEIMAR REPUBLIC) IN THE 1920S AND, IN RECENT HISTORY, ZIMBABWE. ALTHOUGH HYPERINFLATION IS OFTEN ATTRIBUTED TO GOVERNMENTS IRRESPONSIBLY PRINTING MONEY, IT IS USUALLY NOT SO STRAIGHTFORWARD. EXTRANEOUS CIRCUMSTANCE CAUSED BY TOO MUCH INTEREST ON DEBT AND MANIPULATION OF CURRENCIES ON THE OPEN MARKET ARE WHAT OFTEN SPUR HYPERINFLATION.

Unfortunately, financial meltdown just means it will be reorganized by the very people who failed to fix it in the first place. On the other side of the reorganization, America and dollars may be a lot different. Dollars could even be succeeded by a regional or global currency.

WHAT TO DO?

The system is not sustainable. There is really no happy medium. But the only real hope of overcoming the system is knowledge. If enough people had ample knowledge of the system, we could set to work replacing it with debt-free money immediately. And before long, we could become a debt-free country.

However, instead of worrying about a systemic change that may never come, you can take some simple actions today to limit your exposure to the deficiencies and exploitations of the debt system.

HAVES AND HAVE NOTS

Fortunately, other than at the collective government level, no one ever forces people to go into debt; it is ultimately a choice. However, it is also often a choice of necessity. The debt system is dense. Keeping up with the debt world often means being sucked into the debt game. That can be bad news if a person messes up. A poor credit rating can sometimes keep a person from getting a decent job. Without a decent job, it is hard not to go into debt. It is a catch-22, and it is what often separates the haves from the have nots. Mindless institutions lending invented money get to determine people's financial fates. Acting as an obedient slave and building good credit allows a person to become a mini debt master of sorts, with access to ample credit. On a national scale, the entire country has survived many years on having what amounts to a good credit rating. But the whole country is slipping into the same fate as an individual with bad credit.

Sadly, most people have been so well conditioned into accepting the debt system without question that the system seems perfectly reasonable to them. But it is insanity, not reason; it assumes that credit should be a necessity of life. In a sane world, credit would merely be a tool for emergencies.

CIVIL DISOBEDIENCE

The debt system is the kind of thing that demands some civil disobedience. By being smart and disciplined (and having a clean credit slate), you can, for the most part, free yourself from the system altogether by simply refusing to participate in it. To do that, all you really need to do is save enough money to avoid debt and, in turn, hedge your savings.

 ## STEP ONE - SAVE

Do you really need a fancy, pretentious, expensive car when a cheaper, used car can get you from point "A" to point "B" just as quickly? Do you really need a fancy, pretentious, expensive cup of coffee each morning, or an expensive monthly cell phone bill so you can text people while crashing your expensive car? If you can afford that stuff without facilitating debt, that is great. But if you can't, opt to save money. The modern economy is very much built around people spending most of their money instead of saving most of it. But you don't have to play that game.

STEP TWO - HEDGE

Unfortunately, savers are penalized by the hidden tax of inflation. Consequently, if you are going to save money, you need to know where to put it. You usually don't want it just sitting in a bank earning measly interest. And you especially don't want more than $100,000 in any one bank. Banks become insolvent from time to time, and your money is only guaranteed by the FDIC (Federal Deposit Insurance Corporation) by so much.

 ## HOUSING

The first thing you might want to do is put your savings into a place to live. Preferably, you have enough savings to afford a place to live without going into debt. Otherwise, consider just renting. As long as you don't buy during a bubble, buying a place to live should act as a decent store of wealth (since it is a "hard asset" as opposed to a "paper asset"). A house comes with costs like property taxes, insurance, utilities, and maintenance. But since you need a place to live anyway, storing value in your house is a decent deal.

 PAPER INVESTMENTS

So, what happens after you park your savings into a house and you start accumulating more savings? Well, you'll need to put that money somewhere. You could buy something like land if the price is right. Productive land, like potential farmland, is a good thing to have. However, the hyped-up place to put money is the stock market. Yet, while stock is basically a kind of money backed by a company's profit potential, it is still just a transitory paper asset. When measured by indexes (like the Dow Jones Industrial Average) stocks seem like a good long-term investment. But the thing you don't see in indexes is that the stocks that make up indexes come and go. When a company starts to falter or goes outright bankrupt, it is replaced by a new stock. So, buying and holding single stocks for the long run is a recipe to lose your money eventually. Instead, you have to buy and sell cautiously to avoid holding worthless stocks (worthless paper assets). However, the more you buy and sell, the more money you end up giving to middlemen.

STOCKS THAT MADE UP
THE DOW JONES INDUSTRIAL AVERAGE
1929, 1979, 2008

JANUARY 8, 1929	JUNE 29, 1979	FEBRUARY 19, 2008
ALLIED CHEMICAL	ALLIED CHEMICAL	3M
AMERICAN CAN	ALUMINUM CO OF AMERICA	ALCOA
AMERICAN SMELTING	AMERICAN CAN	AMERICAN EXPRESS
AMERICAN SUGAR	AT&T	AIG INC.
AMERICAN TOBACCO B	AMERICAN TOBACCO B	AT&T
ATLANTIC REFINING	BETHLEHEM STEEL	BANK OF AMERICA
BETHLEHEM STEEL	DU PONT	BOEING COMPANY
CHRYSLER	EASTMAN KODAK	CATERPILLAR
GENERAL ELECTRIC	EXXON CORPORATION	CHEVRON
GENERAL MOTORS	GENERAL ELECTRIC	CITIGROUP
GENERAL RAILWAY SIGNAL	GENERAL FOODS	COCA-COLA
GOODRICH	GENERAL MOTORS	DUPONT
INTERNATIONAL HARVESTER	GOODYEAR	EXXON MOBIL
INTERNATIONAL NICKEL	INCO	GENERAL ELECTRIC
MACK TRUCK	IBM	GENERAL MOTORS
NASH MOTORS	INTERNATIONAL HARVESTER	HEWLETT-PACKARD
NORTH AMERICAN	INTERNATIONAL PAPER	HOME DEPOT
PARAMOUNT PUBLIX	JOHNS-MANVILLE	INTEL CORPORATION
POSTUM INCORPORATED	MERCK & COMPANY, INC.	IBM
RADIO CORPORATION	MINNESOTA MINING & MFG	JOHNSON & JOHNSON
SEARS ROEBUCK	OWENS-ILLINOIS GLASS	J.P. MORGAN CHASE
STANDARD OIL (N.J.)	PROCTER & GAMBLE	MCDONALD'S
TEXAS COMPANY	SEARS ROEBUCK	MERCK
TEXAS GULF SULPHUR	STANDARD OIL OF CALIFORNIA	MICROSOFT
UNION CARBIDE	TEXACO INCORPORATED	PFIZER
U.S. STEEL	UNION CARBIDE	PROCTER & GAMBLE
NATIONAL CASH REGISTER	UNITED TECHNOLOGIES	UNITED TECHNOLOGIES
WESTINGHOUSE ELECTRIC	U.S. STEEL	VERIZON
WOOLWORTH	WESTINGHOUSE ELECTRIC	WAL-MART
WRIGHT AERONAUTICAL	WOOLWORTH	WALT DISNEY

 # PRECIOUS METAL

There is a general rule that basically says that any competent person has about 10 percent, or more, of his or her savings in physical gold. You probably don't want to buy gold (or other precious metals) when the price has just shot way up. However, if it stays there, then that is probably the new price to buy. Precious metals, particularly gold, tend to be a good store of value over time. Gold is still the international standard for "real money."

The quantity of gold is limited, unlike the quantity of paper money. So, gold acts as a good inflation hedge.

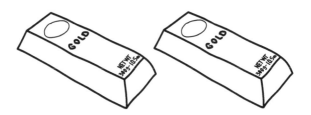

IF YOU CAN'T BEAT THEM, JOIN THEM

There is no denying that you can make a lot of money using the leverage afforded by debt. You can use debt to extract money from the system in many ways. In the stock market, you can buy stock on margin or use options. With commodities, you can trade futures. With banking, you can get entrepreneurial loans. And basically, anything you can do to get money through involvement with the government means capitalizing off of debt. The government is trillions of dollars in debt. So, any money it spends while not paying down the debt is only sustaining the debt.

Ultimately though, by joining the debt game, you end up perpetuating the debt insanity. Plus, you can also lose a lot of money playing with debt.

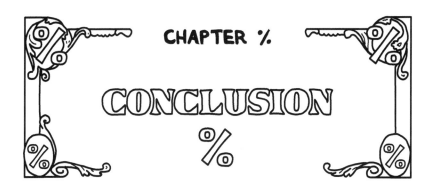

CHAPTER %

CONCLUSION %

Dollars are dissolving because dollars today are paper assets backed by nothing but debt (IOUs). Paper assets without anything tangible behind them dissolve into nothing sooner or later. Dollars may have a good week, or year, where they seem to slow their dissolving—especially when compared to other dissolving, debt-ridden paper currencies around the world. However, the trend ever since the inception of the Federal Reserve System is quite clear, dollars *are* dissolving. To keep up with interest bearing debt, their supply is steadily (sometimes rapidly) expanding, resulting in eroding purchasing power.

The current economy is built upon an unprecedented experiment. The United States doesn't even make much of anything anymore except debt; it is a phony service sector economy that consumes rather than produces. That is a recipe for an unsustainable economy. Many of our brightest minds, instead of going into useful things like engineering and science, are sucked into the lucrative world of finance (as well as things like law). So, instead of using their minds for innovation, they use their minds to make sense of things like Keynesian economic theory and become parasitic debt jugglers.

People worried about things like socializing healthcare, saving social security, war, the environment, education, etc. would do well to look beyond those surface problems and instead first focus on the fundamental problem. The fundamental problem comes before all those other problems. The fundamental problem is the debt monetary system (combined with the public's unconsciousness concerning its workings). The debt system must be replaced with a debt-free system. Otherwise, all the things people try to do to fix the problems that aren't the real fundamental problem will simply add fuel to the already roaring fire.

Implementing debt-free money (and honest banking) is as much a matter of practical economics as it is a matter of preserving (restoring) liberty. Only a small group of people would ever buy into this insanely abstract system that we have today if it was proposed in detail as a replacement for our current system. And yet, it is the system we have today. As time passes, the past debts of the system will simply continue to stack up to be dealt with at a later date. As this giant stack of debts grows taller and becomes ever more vulnerable to random waves of calamity, the government will grow ever larger in its indebtedness to try blocking the waves. Perhaps the system can survive with modifications, but it will be at the sacrifice of America's economic status.

FUTURE

Modern economics is a spectacle of abstract excess. Sooner or later abstraction meets reality and the fatal flaw of modern debt-based money boils to the surface. Today, accompanying the debt problem are many other problems: energy, the environ-

ment, resource scarcity, out-dated infrastructure, terrorism, and ultimately war.
In the coming years, those problems, and
more, will weigh heavily on the economy.
It is going to be a bumpy ride. Finding a
realistic, long-term, sustainable solution
will first require establishing debt-free
money.

Debt-free money is the moral of this
story. However, until money becomes debt-
free, it's all about dissolving dollars. So,
come on! Help stop the doomed, ignorant
enslavement of America (and the world) to
parasitic banking and debt by sharing this
knowledge with as many people as possible.

Alex

130

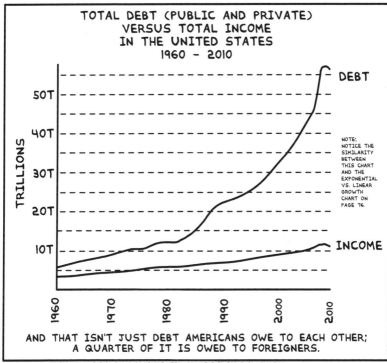

132

References and Suggestions for Further Reading

*Brown, Ellen H. <u>Web of Debt: The Shocking Truth About Our Money System and How We Can Break Free.</u> Baton Rouge, LA: Third Millennium P, 2008.

El-Diwany, Tarek. <u>The Problem with Interest.</u> London: Kreatoc Limited, 2003.

Fischer, David H. <u>The Great Wave: Price Revolutions and the Rhythm of History.</u> New York: Oxford UP, 1997.

Greider, William. <u>Secrets of the Temple: How the Federal Reserve Runs the Country.</u> New York: Simon & Schuster, Incorporated, 1989.

*Griffin, G. Edward. <u>The Creature from Jekyll Island: A Second Look at the Federal Reserve.</u> New York: American Media, 1998.

Howe, Loren. <u>The Real Story of Money, Health, and Religion.</u> Morrisville, NC: Lulu Press, 2006.

Paul, Ron. <u>The Revolution: A Manifesto.</u> Grand Rapids: Grand Central, 2008.

Rothbard, Murray N. <u>The Case Against the Fed.</u> Annapolis: Ludwig von Mises Institute, 1994.

Schiff, Peter D., and John Downes. <u>Crash Proof 2.0: How to Profit From the Economic Collapse.</u> 2nd ed. New York: Wiley, 2009.

*<u>The Secret of Oz.</u> Dir. William T. Still. DVD. 2009.

Von Mises, Ludwig. <u>Human Action: A Treatise on Economics.</u> Little Rock: Fox & Wilkes, 1997.

* Vrabel, Damon. <u>Renaissance 2.0.</u> Online Video. csper.org. 2010.

* The Most Directly Pertinent

About the Author

Alex is a perpetual student, an artist, and a private investor. His investing and economic philosophy expands from the Austrian School of Economics.

DISSOLVING DOLLARS

Visit the Dissolving Dollars website online at
www.dissolvingdollars.com

Made in the USA
Lexington, KY
17 September 2011